THE HAND

FROM

A to Z

ABOUT THE AUTHOR

Judith Hipskind Collins has studied palmistry since 1967. She works as a professional palmist in Dallas, Texas, conducts private research, teaches and lectures, and does programs for both small groups and corporations. She is the author of *Palmistry: The Whole View* and *The New Palmistry*.

TO WRITE TO THE AUTHOR

If you wish to contact the author or would like more information about this book, please write to the author in care of Llewellyn Worldwide and we will forward your request. Both the author and publisher appreciate hearing from you and learning of your enjoyment of this book and how it has helped you. Llewellyn Worldwide cannot guarantee that every letter written to the author can be answered, but all will be forwarded. Please write to:

Judith Hipskind Collins
c/o Llewellyn Worldwide Ltd.
P.O. Box 64383, Dept. 0-7387-0756-2
St. Paul, Minnesota 55164-0383, U.S.A.

Please enclosed a stamped, self-addressed envelope for reply, or $1.00 to cover costs.
If outside U.S.A., enclose international postal reply coupon.

Many of Llewellyn's authors have websites with additional information and resources. For more information, please visit our website: http://www.llewellyn.com.

The HAND *from* A to Z

THE ESSENTIALS OF PALMISTRY

Featuring 185 Illustrations & Unique
Dictionary of Character Traits

Judith Hipskind Collins

Llewellyn Publications
St. Paul, Minnesota

First Edition
First Printing, 2005

Book interior design and editing by Connie Hill
Cover design and interior illustrations by Ellen Dahl

Llewellyn is a registered trademark of Llewellyn Worldwide, Ltd.

Library of Congress Cataloging-in-Publication Data pending

Llewellyn Worldwide does not participate in, endorse, or have any authority or responsibility concerning private business transactions between our authors and the public.

All mail addressed to the author is forwarded but the publisher cannot, unless specifically instructed by the author, give out an address or phone number.

Any Internet references contained in this work are current at publication time, but the publisher cannot guarantee that a specific location will continue to be maintained. Please refer to the publisher's website for links to authors' websites and other sources.

Llewellyn Publications
A Division of Llewellyn Worldwide, Ltd.
P.O. Box 64383, Dept. 0-7387-0756-2
St. Paul, MN 55164-0383, U.S.A.
www.llewellyn.com

Printed in the United States of America

CONTENTS

PREFACE

Palmistry is an art that requires powers of deduction and a clear grasp of the nature of the hands themselves. As an extension of the brain, hands never reflect isolated or random traits, but rather the whole person: the spirit and motivation, the personal needs and temperament of every individual.

Understanding all these areas through an analysis of the hands—the zones, texture, flexibility, fingers, shapes, mounts, and the lines—provides a unique basis for a deeper awareness of ourselves and others.

This book is dedicated to fostering that awareness, and to palmistry as a living art that needs excellent and sensitive palmists to bring it to completion.

1

The World of Hand Analysis

*P*erhaps the biggest surprise about palmistry, especially for beginners, is the amount of detail involved in decoding the hands' meaning. Contrary to the common idea that palmistry concerns only the lines in the hand, a good analysis requires much more. Lines are at their best when they are supported by all the features in the hand.

To get the whole picture, lines must be analyzed together with areas of the palm known as mounts, with the length of the palm and fingers, and the shape of the fingertips and nails. Each hand has a certain shape and thickness, as do the fingers. Each hand has its own consistency, feeling soft or hard to the touch. Each set of fingers has an overall flexibility, and every finger has its own unique degree of flexibility.

How do we add up all these features and draw a picture of a person from the hands? The complete approach to reading hands is outlined in the first half of this book. An explanation is given for all the features found in the hands.

However, some readers may want to go directly to the Dictionary of Traits to read about personality traits revealed by the hands, without learning the whole subject of palmistry. If you are one of those readers, whether you are a beginner or a pro, you will benefit from a review of all the points entailed in a complete hand analysis, as presented in the first half of this book.

But first, there are two keys to successful work with the hands. The ability to be observant is one of them. What better way to start a hand analysis than to notice a hand's size or width or length? Even though a beginner might say, "How do I know if I'm seeing a big hand or a little one, a thick hand or a thin one?" just a few minutes spent looking at a few pairs of hands will instantly reveal obvious differences such as size and shape.

The second key to successful hand analysis is an ability to compare and contrast each feature you see. Which hand is bigger? Looking at two sets of hands at once, you can compare them, but if you happen to look at the hands of one person at a time, you will need to carry a mental image in your head of what you have seen before. That's rather like being a good card player and remembering what card was just played. That very card, if you can recall it, might seal your strategy in the game. So, too, with hands. Anything you can remember of what you have seen before will increase your skill as a hand analyst.

Another valuable tool in the world of hand analysis is a system to organize all the clues you find in a hand. The order in which you deal with all the hand's features can be very important. The lengthiest analysis of hands starts with the back of the hands, if you use the system presented in this book. With a shorter analysis, such as looking up individual traits in the dictionary, the order of the clues is still important, as we will see in the Guide to the Dictionary. Before you do that, let's look at the summary of the long way to analyze hands.

COMPLETE SYSTEM OF ANALYSIS

To get the more obvious clues first from the hands, have your clients put their hands down on a flat surface in order to allow you to see the backs of their hands. This is the order of what you will notice (the page numbers in parentheses tell you where to find a diagram that illustrates that feature):

Body Language of the Hand

1. The spacing between the two hands as they rest on a table (p. 30).
2. The spaces between the fingers (p. 29).
3. The alignment of the thumbs (p. 30).

Nails

4. The length and width of the nails (p. 38).
5. The shape of the nails (p. 38).
6. The color underneath the nails (p. 34).

Texture

7. Touch the back of your client's hands to determine if the skin is smooth, medium, or coarse in texture.

Flexibility

8. Lift up your client's hands and check the flexibility of the fingers, where they join the palm, at the fingertips, and at the thumb to see if the thumb moves easily or is stiff (p. 46).

Posture

9. Have your client hold his or her hands up. Notice whether all the fingers stand straight or do some of them bend inward or outward?

Divisions of the Palm

10. To understand a larger view of the palm's areas, divide the palm in half, with a line running down the middle of the middle finger to the bottom of the palm. The thumb half of the palm represents a person's conscious energy, and the little finger half represents a person's unconscious energy. This information becomes useful when you look at the individual areas of the palm called mounts (p. 107).

These ten points give you a solid foundation for understanding the hands. With them, you have already uncovered much about the person you are analyzing. You are ready to proceed to the palm itself. Next you determine:

11. The shape of the palm (p. 68).

12. The size of the palm, its thickness or thinness (p. 68).

13. The shape of the fingertips (p. 73).

14. The overall length of the fingers (p. 91).

15. The size of the fingers, whether they are thick or thin (p. 75).

16. The length of the fingers' three sections (the phalanges) (p. 90).

17. The length of each individual finger (p. 91).

The Mounts

The mounts and their marks are powerful guides to a person's temperament, energy, and talent. If you understand the mounts, you have an expert view of a person's potential. Where that potential will lead is the question, and the answer is in the lines.

18. The mounts or individual areas of the palm (p. 107).

19. The marks on the mounts (p. 108).

The Lines

Lines play a unique role, defining character, temperament, energy, and health, as the other features do. The lines are also used to project events on a life path and the shape that path might take.

20. The marks found on the lines (p. 118).

21. The lines themselves, their appearance and their variations (p. 118).

The Major Lines

22. The Life Line. We begin with the life line because every hand has one. Warning: No life line predicts length of life. See page 122 to find out what a "short" life line means. The life line is a visual graph of much of our life path (p. 131).

23. The Head Line, an indicator of talent and how you think (p. 154–157).

24. The Heart Line, a guide to emotions and health (p. 141–145).

25. The Fate Line, a clue to your resources and what you want to accomplish (p. 164–167).

The Minor Lines

26. The Apollo Line, a singular mark of creativity and a rewarding life (p. 174).

27. The Mercury Line, an aid to business ability and health (p. 174).

The meanings for all of the items in this outline are found in the front part of this book. If you master all of them, you will have the equivalent of a Ph.D. in palmistry!

You can choose to focus on just a few of the features in this outline and still get a remarkable portrait of the person you are reading. You can decide what you want to know: What area of life experience is of most interest to you in this person's hands? Do you want to know if the person is a good friend, if the person would be a good mate? Are you compatible with this person? Would this person make a good teacher, boss, or colleague? What is this person like? Energetic or not, determined or not, ambitious or not, loving or not? You can discover any of this in just a few steps by using only the ten points below to analyze their hands.

THE BASICS

Palmistry is not so mystical a subject as some might suppose. Think about this: every object in the world has a size, a shape, a length, and a color. Consistency, texture, and flexibility play their role, too. Consider the following basic points for a moment.

- Size
- Shape
- Length
- Color
- Consistency

- Texture
- Flexibility
- Mounts
- Lines
- Gestures

Examples of these features in everyday use include the fact that size, shape, length, and color tell you whether you are looking at an elephant or a lion. Consistency lets you know whether dinner is undercooked or overcooked. Texture defines a rough or smooth piece of cloth, while flexibility helps you decide whether a curtain rod is strong enough to hold heavy drapes.

A hand's size reveals the lens through which you view the world—focusing on the big picture or on the gritty details. A hand's shape and length refer to various types of temperament, as does color. Color, however, goes further, and speaks about your energy, momentum, and health, and highlights the active, progressive areas of your life. The consistency of your hand also offers a commentary on your health and momentum. The texture of your skin seen on the back of the hand shows the degree of sensitivity with which you approach the world, and it also diagnoses your stamina. Flexibility in a hand acts as a straightforward indicator of that very trait in your personality. In palmistry, gestures refer to how you hold your fingers as you use your hands. Your hands in motion as you go about your everyday tasks reveal clues to your feelings and needs. A small list of gestures and their meanings is found on page 188.

When you look at the dictionary and see how these features work to produce a portrait of your personality traits, you will be amazed.

2

What Does Palmistry Do?

How many times have you heard it said, "Your destiny is in your hand"? And indeed it is, but this destiny is not a gift from the powers-that-be, nor is it impossible to alter. The destiny in your hands is nothing more than the record of what you have chosen to be in order to express yourself and fulfill your needs. Destiny in palmistry means choice, and the purpose of palmistry is to help you choose what you want in accordance with what you have already become. Palmistry is an overview of a multitude of options.

Does this sound different from your own idea of palmistry? The popular notion of a reader in a darkly curtained room who asks for your left hand only, who tells you all you wanted to hear, and then some, is such a romantic idea—and so full of misconceptions. Such a situation shouldn't be taken seriously—but it is, for reasons we shall see shortly. Part of the reason such a reading will be taken seriously relates directly to the need the person has to know. The need for guidance is genuine oftentimes, as is the desire for reassurance about the future.

This desire does not have to go unfulfilled, for there is a way to counsel based on the traits in the hands. It lies in an assessment of the past—readily visible in the hands—and the present, both integrated in a smooth flow of an outline of possibilities for the future. Specifically, such counseling is based on a study of inherited traits, vitality, temperament, accomplishments, talents, and needs—all of which can be deduced from the hand.

If we reflect on the stereotype of a palm reading for a minute, it has to be admitted that entertainment is one reason people go to a palmist. Most people will cheerfully say, "It's only for fun," but let's not be fooled. Everyone is vulnerable, for there is a nagging, almost superstitious feeling—prevalent in all of us—that says: if it's in my hand, then it must be so. The instinctive quality of this feeling—and hence its irrational or intuitive basis—is borne out by the fact that few people are neutral about having their hands read. Most are fascinated, be it willingly or reluctantly, and people who have had their hands read know exactly how personal the hands become in that situation. They have experienced the fascination that makes palm reading just a bit easier to believe.

Obviously you should be very careful about whomever you let look at your hands. If a friend of yours wants to, there is a connection already established that is a basis for trust and dialogue, but if you are about to let a stranger look at your hands, you might be well-advised to know some traits that signify a good palmist. No one person must possess all of these traits, but the presence of any one of them is a clue to a reliable reader.

- A good palmist will take both of your hands and study them carefully before saying the first word. This could be a time for you to feel a little uneasy. The feeling of "Oh, oh! What does she see? It must be awful. She isn't speaking. She won't tell me," is a natural reaction, but pausing before speaking is the biggest favor a palmist can do for you, because every second spent in evaluating all the signs in your hands cuts down the possibility of error. Error always comes with the oversight or elimination of an important detail, no matter how tiny it may be. A reliable palmist won't burst out with any definite information the second you hold out your hand.

- A good palmist won't play games or try to guess at the appearance of your lover or your first cousin twice-removed. Nor will he or she speak in ordinary fortune-telling cliches. Surprisingly enough, a good palmist will be asking you questions. Does this surprise you? Questions are asked not because the palmist needs to pull information out of you, but because it's only considerate to get your reaction. That is the spirit in which questions should be asked. If you feel any information is being fished out of you for any reason other than consideration of your feelings, feel free to clam up. Truth and accuracy are the hallmark of a good palmist, and drama should lie only in the marvelous exchange of verifiable information taking place.

- Finally, very often a good palmist will joke with you. This indicates that you are free to take the reading for what it is worth; there is no obligation to swallow it whole. The ability to joke and talk with you, rather than making proclamations as an ambassador of higher powers, tells you that this palmist has an open mind. Most importantly, you will note that the palmist is cautious about demonstrating the ability to see and interpret.

What palmistry can do is in part defined by a list of things it cannot do. Palmistry cannot predict the length of any life, the number of marriages or children. Please don't be disappointed by this. Doesn't this fact actually give you a feeling of relief? The secret of your life's length is your own, and best of all, helpful advice in romance can be given—once you realize that there is no such thing as "x" number of marriages and children waiting to be brought out of the wings by a seer.

"Yes," you say, "but what about all the cases where such predictions came true, and why can't I benefit from a like performance?" Because, if these predictions came true, they came as the result of a flash of intuition, not from signs in the hand, and all such flashes of intuition have the unfortunate drawback of working only some of the time. You might be the casualty rather than the lucky winner in the case of psychic readings.

There are definitely two approaches to palmistry.

The Psychic Approach

This variety uses the hand as a focal point for whatever is floating around in the reader's unconscious. It surely is stunning when the information comes out accurately. One instance is a personal reading in which the reader said, "Oh, I see an airplane ramp in your hand. You will be on an airplane in three days." And so it was. But no amount of staring or close inspection of the hand revealed an airplane ramp. If you choose this approach to palmistry, have fun and be prepared to take a gamble.

The "Book" Approach

For those of you who want something a little more safe and secure, there is always the type of palmistry recorded in books on the market. This approach is the result of a century-and-a-half investigation of old gypsy legends and the application of that research into gypsy legends and folklore. What you get with "book palmistry" is the fun of gypsy lore backed up by traits that have repeatedly and accurately been linked with certain kinds of deductions. If you want to become a reader within this branch of palmistry, you will always have something to say, and will not have to rack your brains just in case your unconscious refuses to be stirred up and divulge secret details. In the case of "book palmistry," the information is all related to character, motivation, personality, talent, interests, and abilities. These subjects in themselves make pretty interesting reading.

A thorough reading can detect and define the kind of energy available for carrying out all the possibilities that are seen in the hand. In fact this is one of the single most important services of palmistry: to allow a complete analysis of the resources a person has and to make it clear how these resources should be distributed and developed, all with an eye to fostering individual potential.

Here is an example of a reading that can increase awareness of personal potential through pointing out an obstacle to that potential:

> An analysis of a young person's hands shows that this person has definite potential as an artist. There is a great depth of emotional perception that adds to technical skill and feeds the artistic sense. However, there is an obstacle. There are signs that this person wastes time in unproductive daydreams because a desire for escape has been allowed to take the upper hand, superceding the will to produce. At this point, the palmist would speak frankly of this tendency to daydream rather than act, and the palmist would pause a moment to assess the listener's reaction. If this person readily admits daydreaming, then it is possible to explain the cause as it exists in the hand (the desire for escape). If the listener seems to be unaware that her or his daydreams are leading nowhere, then a cautious and firm confirmation of the reading suggested by the hands may rattle self-awareness in a productive way. All this can be done if the palmist is careful and tactful.

Palmistry, because it touches on individual potential and the powers to create a life from this potential, is one of the most important forms of dialogue today. Its importance is intensified by the fact that communication is the crux of everyone's development right now. Palmistry, because it is a means to understanding one's self and to understanding another, stands ready to do its part in the peaceful evolution of humanity.

WHY PALMISTRY WORKS

Our hands are unique in their connection with the brain. They are the termination point of countless numbers of impulses that travel from the brain as a result of its activity. As such a point, the hands are designed to carry out physical activity. Through constant interplay with the muscles, these nerve endings leave traces in the hands known as the "lines." To understand what the lines are all about, it is important to grasp the fact that the lines are a result of brain-directed activity. Speech, which records our thoughts for others to hear, is a motor function. The thoughts that are the substance of our speech are transmitted through the motor function of speaking. In much the same way, thoughts that are the result of our desires, hopes, and attitudes are transmitted through the lines on the hands—lines that are but a record of the brain-directed activity of the hands. The direct relationship between brain and hands is one reason why palmistry works.

Hands are said to reflect character and personality. In the first chapter we saw that a century and a half of research stands behind most of the written interpretations of the hand. This research is a second reason why palmistry works.

A third reason will be found in medical annals. Medicine examines the hands for certain signs of health: the nails, the shape of the fingers, the color of the hands—all have a bearing on the condition of the body. In one specific instance, a certain deformed shape of the little finger is associated with cretinism or thyroid deficiencies. The connection between hormones and behavior is well known. The mere association of a certain shape of one finger with a hormonal imbalance leads to the inescapable conclusion that the shapes of the fingers do have some relationship with hormones—and consequently with behavior. There is no medical basis for the entire scheme of temperament as defined by the shape of fingertips in palmistry, but an opening exists. This opening could, with proper research, lead to yet another way of validating palmistry: medical research.

The skin ridge patterns in the hand are hereditary and have traditional meanings in palmistry. Medical science is discovering that alterations in the normal patterns are part of a group of clues to birth defects. Medical science is definitely a potential source of further knowledge about the significance of the hands.

Tests of the effects of sensory deprivation are yet another interesting sidelight to the study of lines in the hand. Students put in a dark room, unable to move or use their senses, were allowed only to hear a bell. At the sound of the bell, the students were to think of certain activities and to think of these activities in a prearranged order. As a student thought of playing basketball, for instance, the appropriate muscles registered a response, even though the student was prone and inert. The purpose of this study was to demonstrate that perhaps the fatigue that comes from studying is not just mental strain. It seems too that the muscles are responding to what is being read or seen, however subliminally.

This same action or reaction exists in the hand. From time immemorial it has been asserted that the nerves' activities make a "groove" in the palm. This assertion is all the more credible when seen in the light of the above experiment. The hand is an endpoint for impulses from the brain. Thoughts that are held over a long period of time, attitudes that are part of a person's outlook or needs, are bound to activate sensory responses in the hands—which responses, in turn, register as "lines."

The question immediately comes to mind: if this is so, then the lines must change, since no one's thoughts are constant and unchanging. Our desires change from time to time—absolutely so—and as the changes occur, new lines are formed or old ones are modified. Any number of changes occur in the hand, but there is a certain set of lines, known as the major lines, that is least likely to change.

That is because these lines (heart, head, and life lines) are hereditary and formed in the first sixteen weeks after conception. Genetics, rather than a response to the environment, controls the appearance of these lines for the most part. However, minor changes are recorded right on these lines, indicating the ravages of time— "ravages" because it takes an unusual set of circumstances to mark or change, however little, any of the major lines, and changes are usually the result of trauma or a forced need to adapt to a pattern of behavior that is not native to the person.

A close look at just a few hands will tell you that the number of lines in a hand can be staggering. If only three have slight changes, that in no way detracts from the fact that lines change. Every other line in the hand is subject to change throughout the lifetime. Changes come as a result of our response to our environment — including our stay in the womb. This is why babies are born with many lines on their hands, or at least more than the three major hereditary lines.

Evaluation of the major lines and all the remaining lines suggests a contrast between what is "given" or inherited and what is accomplished by the person.

Palmistry works because the lines are an interplay between genetics and the environment.

3

So You Want to Be a Palmist?

*M*any people would like to get a glance into the future, or at least into the character of their friends. Curiosity is always the first motivation, and this trait is a good beginning for the study of palmistry, but curiosity alone isn't sufficient; so much more is needed.

Even though there are a variety of reasons for reading hands, all approaches to palmistry need to be marked by certain characteristics.

If these qualities sound a little serious, that's as it should be, for looking at another's hand is a serious business.

Having a definite system to follow during a reading is the best safeguard there is. If you are willing to follow a system that works for you, you will be a good palmist.

Many people express their dismay: "There's so much to remember!" Exactly. That is why a system helps. A structured reading is easier to give and to receive. Chapter four will give you a system to use, as a start.

There are these remaining qualities to be considered, once you agree that a system is helpful and necessary.

- Are you tactful?
- Do you care very much what the other person is thinking and feeling?
- Are you cautious?
- Do you have the ability to not get carried away with your discoveries?
- Do you enjoy a genuine dialogue with the other person, and are you prepared to receive as much input from him or her as possible?

Clearly, an ability to make deductions, an insight into and a sensitivity to others' moods, a sense of courtesy, and a genuine interest in people all help. A feeling for drama and a recognition of the mystery of life are good accompanying traits. If you don't have these last two qualities when you set out to become a palmist, it is a good bet you will before you are through! The study of palmistry can be overwhelming, but it is a good idea to take it step by step, slowly and cautiously. The glow of the drama is your reward for all your tact and caution.

THE NEED FOR CAUTION

Moments ago, we were considering the need for tact, care, and caution in palmistry. To carry the consideration just a bit further, pretend for a moment that you are going to have your own hands read by a professional palmist.

Try to imagine what you feel as you are on your way to meet the reader. Doesn't the feeling involve a little dread and a lot of anticipation? You feel, "Oh, I may not want to hear it all!" This feeling, although it betrays a bit of anxiety, is exactly what makes you continue on your way. You know you are actually eager to hear all the details, yet at the same time you sure hope you don't hear anything too dire.

This dread makes your mind do a funny thing: it gets ready, even though you are not aware of this process, to interpret and use in its own way what the palmist will say. After the reading, then, some doubt may creep into your recall of what was said, and your mind might just construe the palmist's words to mean something they did not.

Somehow, in the process of a reading, things tend to get magnified: whatever good indications came from the reading are blown up into fact; and the not-so-cheery aspects become blown out of proportion.

Both you and the reader will benefit from a clear, systematic reading that makes it easier to recall what actually was said. When you are on the receiving end it is easy to appreciate the need for caution and clarity, but just wait until you are on the other end; it becomes necessity.

There are tricks to the trade that ensure good communication, and as mentioned in the first chapter, the art of asking questions is among them. As a palmist yourself, you will have to learn to ask just the right questions at the right time. To do this, you have to be able to grasp your client's reaction and calculate your next step accordingly. This ability is to be applied for the sake of accuracy and honesty, not for the sake of any possible deception, although this hardly needs repeating at this point.

Here is an example of how this ability to provoke a reaction from a client can make a good reading. You are reading the hands of a woman you don't know. She is a total stranger, and you guess she must be about twenty-five years old.

Immediately, you note in her hands that she has a conflict. It involves her doubting her ability to be a leader and to project herself. This is the starting point of the reading, and because you are not doing a psychic reading and are not going to tell her straight out that she has a conflict, you need to see how to proceed in order to bring out the best in her. You don't know what her present situation is or how she feels about it specifically. The leadership conflict could be happening in any of several partnership situations. While the rest of the hand will help you determine which type of situation is affected by this person's doubt—work, romance, marriage, family difficulties—you still need to know what she feels in order to be tactful about what you see.

So you backtrack in time and, deliberately focusing on a period ten years before (as an approximation), you ask, "Did you enjoy being the leader of the group in high school?" Please note here that you do not tell her that she was a leader in high school. You must listen carefully to her answer to hear how she viewed those days, and indicate, no matter what she says, that you did not mean to tell her she was a leader, but that you are glad to hear her confirm the facts—whether they answer the question "yes" or "no." Her reaction to this question lets you know how she viewed herself in high school, and from this you can get a good idea of how she feels about her leadership ability today. If she has had a negative experience in the past and the traces of that are lingering today in the hand, at least by backtracking ten years you have removed some of the immediate feeling of discomfort that relates to the present. If there is a feeling of regret or discomfort, anger or frustration about that period in her life, then it is best to work on that for awhile. A sympathetic listening from someone who is in a position of knowledge—that's you—will go a long way toward healing.

If the woman says that she loved being a leader in high school and proceeds to give you an account of all her activities, your mind should be working ahead to the fact that something has gone astray more recently to produce signs of conflict in the hand. Your next question could be asked with the projected assumption (although you know this is not so) that everything is fine today, that the leadership ability, once exercised, is still flowing freely today. Your next question should bear more directly upon the source of conflict. At this point the client is free to reveal or hide her conflict. As a palmist you have an obligation to try to induce an awareness of the sign of conflict you see in her hand, but if there is any undue resistance, then it is best to go on to another area of the reading. The reading, then, is actually determined by the reaction of the client.

This approach is preferable to any other in which a palmist asserts his or her own views over and above the client's willingness to listen.

Palmistry is a very delicate exchange between two people. It is really like a tango, which is complex at the beginning and builds in intensity as it progresses, but along with the growing intensity comes a level of ever-higher awareness and communication—the very soul of palmistry.

4

⁓⁓⁓

Getting Started—The System to Use

*Y*ou will want to analyze both hands, for each hand has its own set of information. A complete picture of the person is not possible without coordinating all that exists in both hands, but in this system there is a difference in the function of each hand, whether the person is right- or left-handed. The difference centers on which hand is used by the person for writing, and therefore is dominant. If you are left-handed, then that is the dominant hand. To keep this distinction in mind throughout the book, interpretations will be given for both hands, and the labels, rather than being "left" and "right," will simply be "dominant" and "other." You will know that the "other" hand refers to the left hand if you are right-handed and to the right hand if you are left-handed. Note that most of the diagrams in this book show the left hand. If you are reading a dominant right hand, simply visualize a mirror image of the diagram.

Potential that is inherited or potential that has not been developed at all is not seen so much in the dominant hand as in the other hand. Whatever a person has accomplished or desires to do can be found in the dominant hand. In a certain sense, the dominant hand is a record of events and attitudes that are more conscious in nature, while the other hand is a record of past events a person will recall only occasionally. The other hand shows a person's reactions in the past, behavior triggered by unconscious needs and inherited traits. Assessing these alone, it is possible to project how the person will react in the future, but there is additional help for your analysis in the dominant hand, which is a clear record of how your client has *already* reacted. The dominant hand should always be considered in your projections for the future. In a very simplified sense, the dominant hand reflects mostly the present, while the other hand embraces the past and the future. This is not a strict guideline but only a view of the two hands' roles. Dialogue with each person will reveal to you how much emphasis to put on what you are seeing in each hand.

Before you can begin to weigh what you are seeing in each hand, you need to know how to proceed in the reading. Presented here is a system that works very well for some people, although it is offered as a guideline only. With time and practice, you will very easily develop your own priorities and choices concerning what you want to look for in a hand. You may be surprised to see that in this system the lines are left till the end. This is because a palmist needs every bit of help he or she can get in understanding the lines to the fullest extent of their meaning, and there are many corroborating and qualifying signs in the hand to consider. By becoming acquainted with everything but the lines as a preliminary, you will be prepared to do justice to the lines.

Try this system and see how it works for you:

- **Spaces between the hands and fingers.** Begin your reading by having the client put his or her hands palms down on a flat surface. It should be on a table or area that allows the person to space his or her hands comfortably. Notice what space is left between the hands—are they wide apart?—and what space is to be found between the fingers. There are many variations, and meanings for them are found in the next chapter.

- **Nail shape, skin color and texture, knuckles.** With the hands still palm down, study four things:
  1. the shape of the nails;
  2. the color of the skin;
  3. the texture of the skin on the back of the hands;
  4. the prominence of the knuckles. (Do they bulge at the sides?)

- **Flexibility.** Test the hand for flexibility. Do this by having your client raise his or her wrists upward while the full length of the fingers stays flat on the tabletop. The higher the wrists can comfortably go, the more flexible is the hand. Another way to test for flexibility is to take the client's hand in your own and test how yielding the hand is by pulling the fingers down and away from the palm (see illustration, page 46). Proceed gently. Move the fingertips back and forth at the top knuckle to see how flexible they are. Some tips are amazingly flexible and others scarcely move at all. Try moving the thumb itself and see how easily it gives way. Does it just flop in the direction you pull or does it offer resistance — and how much — to your tugging?

- **Finger alignment, fingertip shape.** Have your client hold his or her hands up in the air, facing you. From this position, notice whether the fingers stand up straight or bend forward. If they bend forward, how much? And which fingers? On which hand? You can also check to see if any of the fingers lean toward each other, or if any of them seem to be turned to the right or left. Notice the shape of the fingertips.

- **Mounts.** Notice the mounts or elevations in the hands while the client's hands are facing you.

- **Lines.** At this point, you are ready to study the lines themselves. Notice the major lines first and then the minor lines. How deeply are they etched in the hand? What are the markings on them? Is there something unusual about anyone of them? You will find that you tend to start with whichever line attracts your attention — probably the one that has the most unusual appearance.

This system provides a useful, flexible framework that can facilitate analysis for both the client and the palmist. It can be readily modified as your knowledge of the art and independence of judgment increase.

5

Between the Fingertips

Spaces speak eloquently. When you think of something spacious, don't you associate the spaciousness with something abundant or elegant? Spaciousness has a lavish connotation, or implies a feeling of freedom, as in the phrase "spacious skies."

Spaces between the hands and spaces between the fingers in palmistry speak of the same abundance, vitality, elegance, and freedom.

The sense of restriction and inhibition associated with narrow spaces or walls also applies to narrow spaces left between the fingers and hands as they rest, palm down, on a tabletop.

SPACING BETWEEN ALL THE FINGERS

When you look at the spaces between the fingers, you are looking for clues to the degree of security a person needs. Everyone experiences the need for security in his or her own way, but what can be seen by the spaces between the hands and the fingers when the hands are resting palm down on a tabletop is the degree to which security needs are being met. Wide spaces show that the need for security is being fulfilled, while narrow spaces betray an insecurity born of a sense of lack or deprivation. Narrow spaces are a defense mechanism in many cases. This is because they indicate a constriction, or a sense of extreme caution, in facing the new and unexpected. "Free spirits" have wide spaces between their fingertips (Diagram A, p. 29—the diagrams for each chapter appear at the end of the chapter).

When you begin your reading by asking the other person to put their palms turned down on a tabletop, you are adding an element of surprise, for few people come to see you expecting to have the backs of their hands read first—or maybe at all! How spontaneously the other person responds to this request can in itself show how he or she reacts to new situations.

Wide spaces always indicate a sense of adventure, a love of the unusual and eccentric. At the same time, they mean that the person is secure enough to experiment with the unknown—or to try a new job, or move to a new location. Wide spaces mean a willingness to experience new things.

Narrow spaces (Diagram B, p. 29) show that the person is very content with things as they are, but the contentment emerges from a "please-don't-rock-the-boat" attitude, not from a sense of genuine fulfillment in their lives.

Moderate spaces (Diagram C, p. 29) mean an average desire for new experiences without the great desire for adventure seen in the wide spaces and without the same need for security indicated by narrow spaces.

SPACES BETWEEN THE HANDS

Wide spaces left between the hands are a sign of readiness for action. This person will act on a moment's notice and think later. The closer together the two hands are brought on a tabletop, the more thought this person puts into his or her actions and projects—before he or she begins. If the two hands actually touch (Diagram D, p. 30), then the person is rather inhibited. If just the two thumbs touch and are aligned perfectly symmetrically (Diagram E, p. 30) with the thumbs extended away from the hand, this shows an unusual degree of tact and consideration. It takes a continual unconscious attitude of consideration for others and an innate sense of precision to bring out this alignment spontaneously.

Try putting your hands far apart on a tabletop, say a card table, as you are seated, and you will notice how this position makes you feel as if you are about to get up from the chair! It is a position ready for action. It is just the way you would put your hands if you were about to get up from the table.

The two hands that touch each other are symbolically leaning on each other. It is a sign the person needs support.

QUALIFYING POINTS

Permanence. All of these qualities we have just looked at in connection with the spaces have something in common: none of them is a permanent sign. The various positions of the hands are easily changed and reflect a current state of mind. What is currently worrying the person, or what is satisfying him or her, is reflected in this spacing. To be sure your clients are putting their hands down with the most natural spacing possible, you can ask them to lift their hands up from the table and put them down again. This gives them a chance to readjust the positions of the fingers if they feel inclined to do so. Note whatever changes occur. They may be important in that they will reflect an ambivalent state of mind if the variation is repeated more than once. If you have your clients raise their hands and put them down several times, you can be very sure of the reading.

Arching. There is another point to look for. When the hands are put palms down, the fingers will either stretch out flat or they will remain curved in an arc (Diagram F, p. 30). If they are curved, the person is feeling uncertain about something. The bigger the arch, the more uncertainty he or she feels—usually about something specific occurring in their life. This deduction will hold true, especially if the arch occurs only on the dominant hand, with the other hand resting flat on the table. If both hands have arched fingers, the feeling of uncertainty is an old and familiar one. You will want to ask this person what it is that he or she is feeling uncertain about. They may want to discuss the matter right away, or you may both want to wait until the reading has gone further.

As we have seen, fingers that remain close together show a person who is not very spontaneous. This person needs structure and order in his or her surroundings to function well. If arched fingers appear in addition to the hands being held close together, there is a problem this person is trying to work out. It no doubt involves a long-standing difficulty or feeling of confusion. Your discussion can bring out aspects of the problem and perhaps set him or her on the way to a solution.

Counterpart traits. Each trait has its counterpart. One not-so-positive trait usually has a side that can contribute to a person's well-being and achievement. This is true with the spaces and their traits. The cautious, formal attitude of close-together fingers also ensures the ability to finish what is started. It means that this person can achieve a great deal if he or she works within a structured environment.

In most cases, a positive sign can have its excesses. It is true that wide spaces reveal a spontaneous person who likes variety and is not bound by conventions, a warm person who feels sympathy with others. It is also true that the need for freedom implied in wide spaces can result in a tendency to take on too many new projects with an inability to finish what is started. Wide spacing between the fingers means that the person must have good self-discipline to realize his or her potential. A narrower field of concentration may be called for. You might advise such a person to pursue some of their personal interests as hobbies rather than as full-time work or preoccupations.

Comparing hands. When you are looking at the spaces and juggling their meanings, you will get good practice at the art of comparing the signs of the dominant hand with the signs of the other hand.

All palmistry deductions are made on the basis of comparing the two hands. Such comparison begins the first second of the reading, and all this mental balancing will have you quite prepared to give a full interpretation to the lines when the time comes.

Note which of the hands lies the flattest or has the greatest arch. Or does neither of them lie flat? Does neither hand have an arch? Although the traits in this case are of a temporary nature, the dominant hand always shows traits that are more recent than are shown in the other hand. Both hands bearing the same signs means an attitude that has gone on for some time.

Spacing Between Individual Fingers

This ability to juggle the meanings and to piece them together accurately for a good reading becomes important as you do the final check for spaces: the spaces between each finger on each individual hand.

All the spaces between the fingers are rarely the same, so these make an easy path for comparison. Take the information from the dominant hand as the trait that currently exists and the information from the other hand as a trait or tendency that is part of the past. This applies only if there is a difference between the two hands. If the spaces between any two fingers on both hands (for example, between the index and middle on both the right and left hands) is the same, then the trait is consistently a part of the person.

Here are the meanings for each possible space:

- **Space between the index and middle fingers**: the ability to think for oneself.
- **Space between the ring and little fingers**: the capability for independent action.
- **Space between the middle and ring fingers**: the need for financial security.

The bigger the space, in the first two instances, the more true is the meaning. With the last space, it is just the reverse. A large space between the middle and ring fingers shows that the person does not worry about their finances, while a small space means money worries.

Differences in the spaces do have an interesting application, and they mark the growth of struggles and achievements.

If the space between the **index and middle fingers** is quite different—a large space on the dominant hand and a small space on the other hand—the person is now thinking more for him- or herself than in the past. The reverse relationship indicates that something currently is blocking or inhibiting the person's desire to think independently. The person may be deferring to a boss over a matter of some importance in the office or trying to compromise in some matter with a partner.

A large space between the **middle and ring fingers** on the dominant hand, accompanied by a smaller space between them on the other hand, means that a person's financial situation is looking up. This person is more disposed to spend his or her money than in the past—usually because there is now more to spend! If the reverse relationship exists—a small space on the dominant hand and a larger one on the other hand—the person has had to cut back on spending. This is an often-seen sign! If the two fingers should touch, there is a strong resolution to not let go of any money unless absolutely necessary. Sometimes this sign, the two fingers held against each other, is carried over into gestures when the hand is not resting on a tabletop, and this means that no matter how good the product, the salesperson might as well save her or his breath and go home. This person is not buying today.

A larger space between the **last two fingers** on the dominant hand and a smaller one on the other hand means that the person is acting more independently than in the past. The reverse position means just the opposite, as in the other spaces.

A checkup, which is often very revealing, concerns the spaces between the first two and the last two fingers. If one is quite different from the other, there is often a momentary conflict apparent. For example, a small space between the index and middle fingers with a large space between the ring and little fingers shows that the person is not thinking for him- or herself, but is acting rather rashly anyway. There is action without thought to back it up. The reverse case also signals conflict: the independent thinking shown in a large space between the first two fingers has no outlet if the last two fingers stay close together. The action is inhibited, but don't be fooled, because what the person is thinking could be a surprise!

SUMMARY

- Fingers close together: a cautious, conscientious person.
- Fingers wide apart: a need for freedom, a sympathetic nature.
- Large space between index and middle fingers: independent thinking.
- Large space between middle and ring fingers: no pressing financial concerns, a disinclination to plan for the future.
- Large space between ring and little fingers: independent actions.
- Small space between index and middle fingers: cautious or inhibited frame of mind. Not open to new ideas.
- Small space between middle and ring fingers: desire to save money, a desire to have a secure future.
- Small space between ring and little fingers: cannot act according to choice, a block to independent actions.

SPACES BETWEEN FINGERTIPS

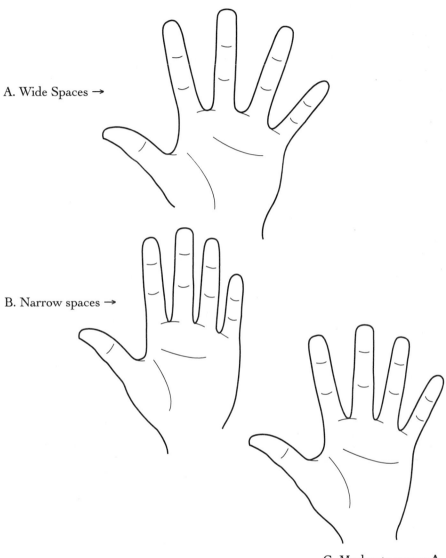

A. Wide Spaces →

B. Narrow spaces →

C. Moderate spaces ↑

POSITIONS OF THE HANDS

← D. Two hands touching

← E. Thumbs aligned symmetrically

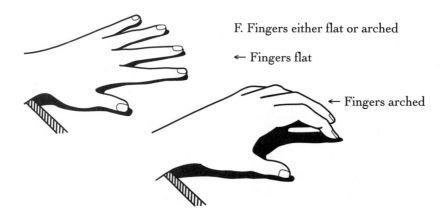

F. Fingers either flat or arched

← Fingers flat

← Fingers arched

6

More Signs from the Back of the Hand

The back of the hand gives more information about your client than you might imagine. It is a rewarding area of study. The main clues you want to scrutinize are: the nails, their shape and color; the color of the skin; the texture of the skin; the shape of the knuckles.

When you get through studying all of these signs, you will have a very good basis for evaluating any other signs in the hand. This knowledge will last and help you for the duration of the reading.

The first of these signs is the nail type, which gives clues both to temperament and physical health.

NAILS

Nails can be categorized in this way: length (long, short, wide, narrow, short and wide, very long—Diagram A, p. 38); shape (oval, square, spatulate, filbert—Diagram B, p. 38); color (red, pink, pale or white, blue).

The length of the nail refers only to the portion that begins at the base and ends at the tip of the finger. The manicured ends are not considered, but only the base and sides.

Ridges in the nails are important clues to health, and these ridges can be either horizontal or vertical (Diagram C, p. 38. Special signs to note are the moons and the presence, if any, of white flecks on the nail.

Long nails (Diagram A, p. 38) are a sign of an easygoing, placid type of person. They show a gentle nature that is not provoked into aggression very often. Such people are perfectionists and put a lot of value on appearances; a love of harmony and beauty is the main reason for this concern for appearances. It is not a vain or superficial emphasis on appearances but a desire for aesthetic, pleasant surroundings and a need to express the self artistically or domestically.

Short nails indicate a more aggressive person (Diagram A), someone who is usually blunt, with a strong curiosity and a need to act.

The width of the nail tells mainly of a person's physical vitality and of his or her approach to life. Wide nails (Diagram A) belong to a more outgoing person. Often, **wide nails** indicate manual dexterity. How many carpenters, for instance, have you seen with narrow nails?

Narrow nails, since they show a lower physical vitality, are found on people who are either quiet or who do not like to take up too many activities at once (Diagram A). If, by chance, you do find a person with narrow nails who is involved in several activities at once, you will often see an exhausted or frazzled person. This person needs quiet and relaxation. All people with narrow nails can benefit greatly from regular physical exercise. If nothing more, it will keep them in shape and on a par with their wide-nail friends.

Short and wide nails (Diagram A) are dynamite! Watch for a very dynamic person whose energy surpasses almost everyone's. The drawback associated with these nails is the need for excellent self-control to channel this excess energy. Short, wide nails always show an exuberant but irritable person. Argumentativeness or aggression "beyond the call of duty" is the result of this sign.

Very long and moderately wide nails (Diagram A) show a person with unusual artistic or creative abilities.

Nail shape is one of the most important guides to the way people like to approach life. The instinctive response to new situations, as well as to daily routine, is mirrored in the shape of the nail. To see the shape, you need to look at the bottom of the nail. The base of the nail will be either oval, square, spatulate, or, in rare cases, filbert (Diagram B, p. 38).

The nails' shape is important as a clue to temperament and behavior. There is a correlation between the shape of the nail and the way a person likes to structure activities.

An **oval nail** denotes a need for conformity in new situations. People who have oval nails tend to be adaptable and to enjoy themselves. **Square nail**s show a need to categorize things, to classify and sort out experiences according to type, rather than to accept events at face value. People with square nails are often meticulous in their appearance or housekeeping and are good at working with their hands. People with square nails like rational explanations, and, above all, an orderly environment.

Spatulate or flared nails belong to a person who asks "Why?"—who needs to explore all the issues. People with these nails seldom can sit still, and they are happiest in situations that call for activity and motion. This type of nail means an inquisitive mind and penetrating insight.

A short sketch of people with each type of nail might be this portrait:

- Round nails: friendly, agreeable, pleasant, and good-humored. He or she doesn't expect too much of others and consequently is not disappointed.

- Square nails: orderly and meticulous by nature, a careful dresser, with close attention to detail; a loyal and dependable friend once involved in a relationship.

- Spatulate nails: eager and anxious, exuberant or perhaps almost overbearing in an urge for activity, quick to explore opportunities; an interesting thinker who loves to talk.

Filbert nails (Diagram B) are a special case. They belong to people who overexert themselves. All people with filbert nails will take on too much to do. The shape is an exaggerated form of spatulate nail. These people are leaders in their own circles. You can count on them to have unusual ideas or to be in correspondence with a wide variety of people. Interest in life is intense. If there is an adventure around the corner, these people usually know. They must be careful to keep up their health and not get carried away with their discoveries or ideas.

Everyone's nails have a characteristic color and, with a little bit of practice, you will be able to distinguish shades of red, pink, pale, or possibly blue nails. Pink nails mean a warm personality and a love of a good time. Such a person is relaxed and healthy and takes her or his pleasure seriously! But **red nails** reflect an excess of the good vitality noted in pink nails; they indicate an irritable or hasty nature. **Pale nails** point to a lower vitality, perhaps lack of good circulation. Psychologically, they show a person who is not outgoing. You would want to weigh this sign against counterbalancing traits in the hand-signs of leadership, for instance. **Blue nails** can mean circulatory problems. If this person smokes, you had better repeat the surgeon general's warning!

There are two common conditions that people often ask about: white spots on the nails and ridges on the nails. The white spots come with fatigue or nervousness, although there is no final answer as to what causes them. **Ridges** are either horizontal or vertical (Diagram C). Horizontal ridges appear on nails after a case of the flu or some other shock to the system. These ridges grow out with the nail, and, since growing time for a nail from base to tip is about six months, you can estimate an approximate time for the event that caused the ridge.

Vertical ridges last longer and do not readily grow out. They do disappear when the condition that accounts for them has been cleared up. Poor digestion is one problem indicated by these ridges. Many people whose systems are not absorbing nutrients properly have these ridges on their nails, particularly the elderly. You might ask about the person's diet when you see vertical ridges. It is a good idea to upgrade nutrition in this case.

SKIN COLOR AND TEXTURE

Coloring in the hand has both a physical and psychological significance. **Pale hands** are associated with introverted and introspective personalities. Such people are often dreamers and have creative personalities. An outgoing and sympathetic person will have a **pink color** in the palm and on the back of the hand. This pink color means good vitality, and there does indeed seem to be truth to the description "in the pink of things"—when you apply it to the hands! **Very red palms** are associated with aggressive or potentially violent people. These people are excitable and have trigger-quick reactions. How they express their emotions can be seen from other factors in the hand. Will-power, conditioning, and environment will have a lot to do with the way their emotional tendencies are handled.

The texture of the skin brings added insight into your client's emotional responses and sensitivity. There is truth, too, to the adage about "thin-skinned" and "thick-skinned" personalities. Hands with perfectly smooth skin, resembling a baby's skin in its fineness, suggest personal sensitivity. Coarser skin that is not a result of chapping or physical labors marks an individualist who is sturdy, vital, and not easily bothered by outside opinion.

Skin texture can be divided into five classes: very fine, fine, medium, coarse, and very coarse.

The visibility of the pores is a good clue to the type of hand you are analyzing. With very fine skin, the whole hand will be so finely drawn that the pores on the entire back of the hand will not be visible. Fine skin has a delicate appearance too, but with this difference: in a small area of the hand, either hair or pores are visible. With medium skin—by far the most common type—there is a smooth appearance, but accompanied by many visible pores. Coarse skin does not have a delicate appearance at all, but looks strong, sturdy, and has readily visible pores. Very coarse skin needs little definition, for it will look and feel rough.

Fineness and coarseness reveal the degree of personal sensitivity. **Very fine skin** means that reactions and responses are swift, possibly hasty, and sink in deep. Experiences are remembered for a long time. **Fine or medium skin** means normal or expected reactions to social and everyday situations, as does coarse skin. The difference between the two types is the degree of personal sensitivity to situations and the environment. **Coarse skin** belongs to a person who can throw off the effects of his or her reactions. They are not easily swayed by emotions. **Very coarse skin** is found on people who are not emotional by nature, but energetic and diligent in pursuing the things they want.

There are other connotations to skin texture. Besides indicating the type of emotional response and the degree of internalization of these responses, skin texture reveals recreational preferences. Fine-skinned people find physical exercise less appealing than coarse-skinned types. Generally, **very fine skin** indicates individuals who never care if they set foot outdoors. This distinction becomes important in choosing a type of job or occupation that will give the greatest satisfaction. **Coarse-skinned** people will never be happy cooped up indoors, nor will they be satisfied with office routine. Fine-skinned people are sedentary by nature. They are happy with indoor pursuits.

KNUCKLES

While your subject's hands remain flat down on the tabletop, there is one last clue to check: look for knuckles that have a bulge (Diagram D, p. 39). The knuckles can bulge at either the top section of the fingers, near the nails, or at the midsection.

These bulges can be spotted just by looking, but sometimes you may want to check further for them by running two fingers alongside each of your client's fingers to see if you can feel a resistance at the knuckles. If your fingers can pass smoothly by the knuckles without any feeling of resistance, then the fingers are called "smooth." Caution is needed here. Knuckle development can be affected both by arthritis and injuries, so ask about this if you think it might be the case. If there is no injury or arthritis to account for the enlarged knuckles, then you have an indication of certain mental qualities.

Smooth fingers denote a mind that works rapidly, like lightning, makes decisions quickly, and is intuitive; at times, they indicate an impulsive person. This person is adaptable.

Large knuckles show a mind that prefers to work slowly and thoroughly, to know all the facts before making decisions. Knuckles like these also mean that the person appreciates an orderly environment. If the knuckles are large at the top of the fingers (Diagram D top), there is a strong tendency for orderly thought. Large knuckles at the midsection (Diagram D bottom) show a person who likes material order and cleanliness. For instance, such people prefer to work at clean counters and like to clear their desks before they sit down to work.

Each type of knuckle shows certain abilities. **Smooth fingers** indicate people with good intuition (Diagram E, p. 39). These are people who can come up with new ideas and whose impressions are quick and straight to the point. Smooth fingers show managerial ability. There is a desire to be up-to-date on all that is new, and these people need to work with others in order to be happy.

Larger knuckles are found on people who love to categorize what they know. They are fond of analysis and classification. Patience is one of their virtues, specifically in the work they do and projects they tackle. Such persons like to finish what they start, no matter how slowly they get the job done. Caution and thoroughness supersede the desire for action.

Key traits of these two types:

- **Smooth fingers:** a lively, quick, and impulsive turn of mind, great or unusual insight, a need to be involved with people.
- **Large knuckles:** a love of order, a need for routine, and appreciation of concrete results.

Interestingly, the admonition "knuckle down" applies exactly to this type!

Knuckle development won't be the same on each finger. Once you have the meanings for each individual finger (chapter twelve and thirteen), those can be further refined by applying what you know about the knuckles. Their development always has a bearing on the way all the traits in the hand function.

In someone with large knuckles, any interest or talent will be expressed with a passion for thoroughness and exactness. Smooth fingers lend an element of liveliness and clever expression to the talents and traits indicated in the rest of the hand.

FINGERNAILS

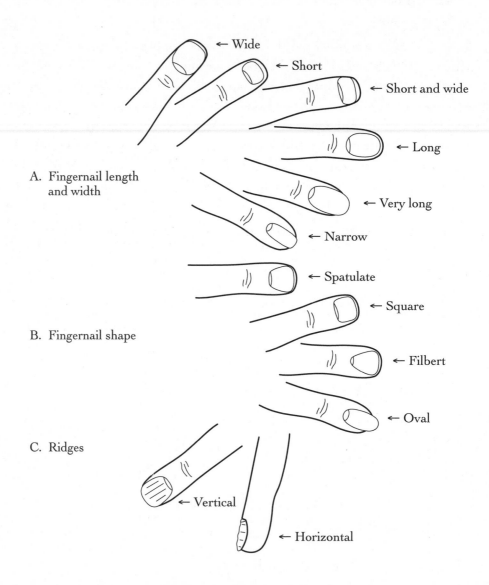

A. Fingernail length
and width

← Wide

← Short

← Short and wide

← Long

← Very long

← Narrow

B. Fingernail shape

← Spatulate

← Square

← Filbert

← Oval

C. Ridges

← Vertical

← Horizontal

FINGER SHAPES

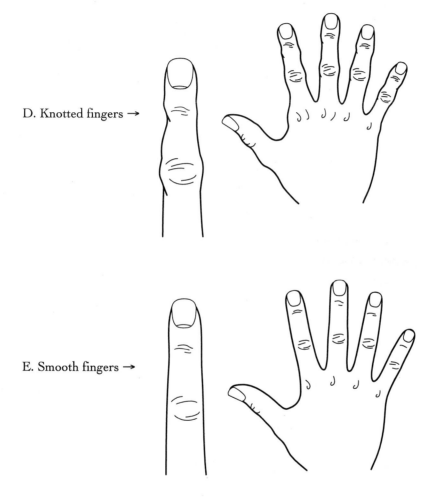

D. Knotted fingers →

E. Smooth fingers →

7

Resistance and Flexibility

*F*lexibility is one of the biggest variables in the hand. There are three areas to be checked on each hand, and each point is likely to have its own degree of flexibility. These three areas are: at the point where the fingers join the palm, the fingertips, and the thumb. Very often, one hand will yield to pressure more easily than the other. Similarly, each fingertip has a degree of flexibility all its own. The best way to test flexibility is to learn to judge the degree of resistance at each of these points in the hand.

Flexibility is considered a positive quality. The main import of a flexible hand is the ability to adapt to change. Whenever a hand is flexible in any of the areas, but most especially in the first listed above, a love of variety and change are indicated. Stiffness in the hands shows a personal viewpoint that is not likely to change. Too much flexibility and too much resistance have the pitfalls appropriate to each extreme: in the first case, there can be a lack of stability and, in the latter, the possibility of trauma and stress accompanying inevitable change and growth.

FLEXIBILITY BETWEEN FINGERS AND PALM

Begin your examination of the hand by having the client raise his or her wrists up while the fingers stay flat on the table (Diagram A, p. 46). The higher the wrist can go, the greater the flexibility at the point where the fingers join the hand. Then take the hand in yours and, bracing the length of your thumb against the fingers, push down (Diagram A). Both of these tests reveal the degree of resistance or flexibility at the point where the fingers join the hand (Diagram A). This is the basic flexibility of the hand.

If the fingers can be moved back easily at this point, this flexibility is a prime indication of an open mind, in addition to a love of travel and change. Contrary to what you might expect, in most cases arthritis has little to do with stiffness at this point in the hand. There are instances where one hand known to have an arthritic condition is actually more flexible than the other hand. This bears out the fact that the mind and mental outlook determine the degree of flexibility here.

Resistance and flexibility change according to the person's current needs. Therefore, comparing flexibility in the two hands is a good barometer of the need for expansion versus that for the status quo. If only the dominant hand is stiff, there is a growing need to be settled in life, which is not actually accomplished at the time. In the reverse position there are signs that past security needs have been met and that the person is able to seek wider horizons.

Stiff fingers show a need for a secure base of operations, and if the person travels, it will always be with thoughts of home tugging at them. "Safety first!" is their motto. While they are not exactly unreceptive to new experiences and ideas, they can't help evaluating everything new in the light of old and trusted ways. There is a streak of cautiousness and stubbornness in the personality. This stubbornness must not be mistaken for an "I'm always right" attitude—this will show up in other areas of the hand—for the cause is usually a direct result of a fear of change. As a palmist you can perhaps point out the wisdom and value of change.

Flexible fingers. Fingers that bend ever so easily mean a person who is enthusiastic by nature and is as easily moved emotionally as the fingers themselves. These people will be volatile and diverse in their emotions. They may need to achieve an inner calm and steadiness to combat a tendency toward flightiness. A change of scene does these people good. Traveling salespeople are well-suited to their jobs if their fingers are flexible, as are navigators, explorers, and others who work in occupations that keep them on the road.

Flexibility is a good guide for occupational counseling. It cuts down or helps to define the area of activity that might interest the client. Suggesting that a client with stiff fingers become a sailor or enter a job where transfers are likely is a waste of time. Nor would the person who has very flexible fingers benefit from a fourteen-hour-a-day research job that required him or her to work alone in the same surroundings every day.

FLEXIBILITY IN THE FINGERTIPS

You and your client can have fun looking at the meanings for each fingertip's flexibility. This is the second area to check carefully, for each fingertip has its own meaning. But before you concentrate on that, you need to know whether or not most of the fingertips are flexible. Or are they stiff and unyielding for the most part? Overall flexibility indicates a very alert mind. Another feature related to flexible tips is a result of quick and total perception: the ability to mimic. Anyone who has very flexible tips will either do deliberate imitations of others or will often unconsciously pick up other people's mannerisms. Stiff fingertips simply mean that the talent for mimicry isn't there. Signs of an alert or quick mind can exist in other areas of the hand and will be confirmed later.

Since each tip's meaning is so specific, these are good readings for parties and entertainment:

- **Flexible index fingertips:** a courteous and tactful person. A reading for this sign could be: "You really know how to deal with the boss when he's in a bad mood—probably at 8:00 AM Monday morning!"
- **Flexible middle fingertips:** someone searching for values in life that will satisfy them. They seek new ideas constantly. You might get by with telling this person "Your library is your best friend," and go on to explain that any new knowledge or experience is appealing because of a great need to know.
- **Flexible tips on the ring finger:** someone with an eye for line. This person notices how a room is arranged, and any changes in a familiar environment register quickly. "When did you last have an uncontrollable urge to straight-

en a picture on someone's wall?" would be a good question for this person. This tip signals ability in design and layout and denotes an almost unconscious talent for arrangement and construction. There is an artistic sense of order.

- **Flexible tips on the little finger:** the little finger is fun to test: if it is flexible, it means that the person is "ear-oriented." Most often this trait translates into the ability to recognize voices instantly, across a crowded room or over the telephone—even if the voice has been heard only once before. The sound of that voice, its inflections and nuances, do not escape the notice of a flexible little fingertip (Diagram B).

Comparing fingertips on each hand. There is just one further refinement to add to your considerations here. Do the flexible fingertips occur on each hand or just on one hand? If flexibility is found on the dominant hand only, the traits have been learned or acquired. If just the other hand is flexible at the fingertips, the qualities outlined for each specific tip exist, but have not been brought into play by the person.

Arthritis can make a difference in these readings, for it makes fingertips stiff. If you suspect this might be the case, ask your client before you share the meanings.

FLEXIBILITY IN THE THUMB

The thumb is an intriguing part of the reading for flexibility. While you have your client's hand and are testing for the flexibility mentioned already, take a detour to the thumb and move it back and forth. Since you are not concentrating on the thumb area, this will take your client off-guard and thus give you an accurate, spontaneous reading.

Flexible thumbs. If the thumb moves back and forth easily, seeming to have little will to resist—some thumbs seem to flop in the direction of the palmist's pull, showing people who can readily have decisions made for them—they are willing to go along with the group or with a partner's wishes. This doesn't mean that the person is incapable of thinking independently. It simply shows an unwillingness to make decisions that will affect others.

Stiff thumbs that relax. Firmer resistance in the thumb marks a person whose mind is made up on most issues. It means a frame of mind that is determined and does not allow too much outside interference. There is a subtle variation in this meaning, however. If a thumb stiffens when it is touched and pushed, but then relaxes a little, this indicates someone who has a strong defense reaction to their environment or when coping with new situations. Once a measure of security is felt, or of certainty, then the person, and the thumb, will relax.

Stiff thumbs. The thumb that is stiff at first touch and remains that way becomes a reliable sign of stubbornness. This type of person may miss some of the fun in life through his or her unwillingness to try new things. At times, a stiff thumb can indicate a narrow or limited viewpoint, probably as a result of a restricted background. The positive quality, in the case of a resistant thumb, is an ability to concentrate and an immunity to becoming scattered in long-range plans.

With time and practice, the various degrees of flexibility will become second nature for you, and you will recognize the variations easily enough.

Flexibility always gives clues to adaptability and the consequent need for security. You will learn through this sign just how willing the other person is to experience new things and how diversified his or her talents and interests are likely to be.

← A. Flexible at the point where the fingers join the hands

← Below—inflexible at the hand-finger hinge

← Flexible fingers can be pulled back

B. Checking for flexibility in the fingertips →

8

Hands Up in
the Air

*J*ust about the time you reach this chapter, you may
feel you have come a long way in your efforts to
learn all the preliminaries of palmistry. Take heart, because
with this section you are entering another level of palmistry—and therefore drawing closer to the essentials of a
complete reading.

When you have your clients put their hands up in the air
for this part of your reading, it will look as if you had just
said, "Stick 'em up!" This approach produces entertaining
readings at parties, for what the fingers mean can be summed
up succinctly and amusingly at the same time.

With this chapter, you enter another level of interpreting
security needs and their degree of fulfillment. You will be
looking to see whether any of the fingers fall forward when
the hand is held in the air. When a finger droops forward, a
lack of confidence is indicated in the area of life the finger
represents. Those meanings we will see in a minute.

A finger's falling into a forward position, out of line with
the rest, is not a sign of relaxation, even though it may seem
so at first glance. Try holding your own hands up in the air,

and if all the fingers stand up straight, deliberately move one or more forward. You will see that it takes an effort to do this, and it may feel unnatural. The position just won't be comfortable unless it is what your fingers want to do of their own accord. This would be true also for fingers that fall forward and are deliberately held straight up.

Looking at the hands as they are held up in the air will give you meanings that reflect traits more unconscious in nature and of longer duration than those you saw indicated in the spaces between the fingers.

Since the meanings stem from needs which are mostly unconscious, either your client will very likely be quite surprised you could see such a thing, or he or she may deny what you see. If you encounter any resistance or reluctance to discuss the meanings, it is better not to press the subject.

The readings are quite interesting and accurate, and they can be studied in the same light as body posture. Just as people who are discouraged will tend to walk with their shoulders sagging, and not even be aware they are walking this way, so the fingers will sag when they are held up in the air. The need for caution must be reiterated here. You cannot be absolutely certain that the meanings for drooping fingers are applicable as stated to each and every person. The same principle applies in the case of poor posture. Perhaps something other than discouragement, poor muscles, or an accident accounts for drooping shoulders. The real significance of the meanings that follow is that they are generally valid, unless unusual circumstances prevail. More than that, they are a very good cue for opening a dialogue with your client that will further an understanding of her or his needs.

You can have your client rest their elbows on the table with their hands up facing you for the reading. This will be more comfortable, as the readings may take some time to digest.

First, a summary of what each finger stands for in this particular type of reading:

- **Index:** leadership ability.
- **Middle:** philosophy and chosen values.
- **Ring:** contentment with the environment and surroundings.
- **Little:** relationship with parents and the opposite sex.

The forward-leaning index finger. If individuals are uncertain about their own leadership, either at home, socially, or in business, their index fingers will lean forward. These people do not feel comfortable with their leadership abilities, nor are they sure of their ability to control situations and circumstances that involve relationships with other people. There is a lack of self-confidence.

An index finger that stands straight tells of personal contentment with one's leadership and shows the ability to adapt in personal relationships. There is little current conflict about such things.

The forward-leaning middle finger. Many people have one or both middle fingers held forward, because a straight middle finger means that these people are convinced they know just what they need and that their search for values is complete, at least for the present. Since it is not easy to feel satisfied with our knowledge nor to be absolutely certain we know which values are the best ones, a drooping middle finger is a common occurrence.

When you see this you can remark that a push to determine what values can best satisfy and fulfill your clients would be to their advantage.

If the middle finger is straight, you know this person has done some inner searching or was satisfied with the moral and social values taught them early in life.

Ring fingers often lean forward, too, because dissatisfaction with environment, signaled by this position, is common. A person with drooping ring fingers feels that her or his environment is limiting in some way, and he or she dislikes the routine it imposes. This feeling will apply to whatever the personal situation entails—a job, schooling, or household routine.

When you see this finger drooping forward, you need to ask your client just what it is about their circumstances that is bothersome, for the possibilities are numerous. You could start by enumerating these possibilities, tailoring them to the obvious age and sex of your client.

A younger person may well be dissatisfied with school. A person who seems to be in their early twenties or older, who is wearing a wedding ring, could be having problems balancing the demands of work with matters that call for attention at home.

If the ring finger stands straight on both hands, then the person is content with their surroundings and with the balance they have achieved in managing their life. It is the sign of a reasonably happy person.

The little finger can be quite a topic of discussion in itself, for its meanings relate entirely to your client's feelings about their parents or the opposite sex. If the finger is straight, all is clear in this area, but if either finger leans forward, you will want to discuss all the reasons that could account for it.

The prime factor is your client's relationship with his or her parents, and what caused any feelings of unhappiness or resentment. These feelings will be buried by now, but do bear looking at and exploration so that the person can get a better view of why she or he acts as they do in personal relationships today.

Many times, needs that weren't fulfilled by the parents are reflected over and over again in living patterns. Roles that were once perceived as acted out by the parents will be adopted by the child. Because this operates on an unconscious basis, those who come on the scene after the initial impression has been made by the parents' behavior, or after the child has arrived at his or her interpretation of that behavior, are often at a loss to understand the adopted behavior. Palmistry in this case can open up a potentially rewarding dialogue. The most serious areas of life can be discussed if the palmist handles the consultation properly, for the very act of seeing something amiss in the hands gives an unusual opening for this exploration of personal needs.

A forward little finger means either that the parents and child did not relate well, although they lived under the same roof, or that one of the parents was physically absent and the lack is still felt by the child.

Unhappy relationships and difficulties with parents seem to produce a later need for approval that is so strong it leaves a burning ambition to achieve—constantly. Thus the same little finger that marks difficulties with parents often presents a very dynamic person!

The need for acceptance in the case of a curving little finger can become an overriding preoccupation, and fulfilling this desire means that the person will bend over backward (similar to the little finger that bends forward) to please others. This includes telling little white lies that might make the other person feel better. So it is possible that a curved little finger will lead to a tendency not to speak the truth at all times; but to read this finger as a sign of blatant dishonesty won't do anyone a favor. It is always necessary to seek out the motivation behind the tendency and to keep in mind the conflicts that may have produced it.

All fingers leaning forward or held straight. Perhaps all the fingers lean forward. Insofar as they do, a corresponding measure of insecurity invades the entire personality, and the person's anxieties are likely to be vague, undefined, or at least more extensive than recognized. Finding the root of this anxiety is quite a job, and it is far from likely that you as a palmist will find it in one sitting, but you can mention the presence of this sign and explore any possible reasons that surface for the anxiety's foothold.

All the fingers held straight in the air are like a robust flag, signaling vitality, contentment, and a harmonious flow of energy.

Fingers leaning to the sides. In another type of curve, the fingers do not lean forward, but to one side or the other of the hand, listing toward either the thumb side or the outside of the hand. If, when the hand is held up in the air, all the fingers slant toward the thumb (Diagram A, p. 53), the person needs to be active at all times to be happy. There is a strong desire for motion that is related to a dynamic or restless state of mind. This also indicates a desire for achievement and a strong sense of purpose in life. When the fingers slant toward the little finger side of the hand (Diagram B, p. 53), there is a more inward turn of mind, a love of contemplation and dreaming.

The lateral curve. The last type of curve is commonly called a "lateral" curve. In this type, the fingers don't bend forward, but the tips themselves are curved, along with part of the finger itself, toward another finger (Diagram C, p. 53). Normally only the index, middle, or little fingers have this curve. On the index finger, when it leans toward the middle finger, such a curve means a serious and dutiful outlook on life. If the curve is exaggerated, then this person's true motives will be hard to know. He or she finds it hard to disclose what they are thinking, especially if it means revealing emotions.

If the middle finger leans toward the index finger, signs of ambition are emphasized, but if this finger leans toward the ring finger, emotions are likely to be inhibited. A ring finger curving toward the middle finger is rare, but if it does, the person has a serious conflict between duty and the pursuit of pleasure. It will be helpful to try and make this person aware that everyone experiences a degree of guilt, and that they must try not to let guilt dominate them to the extent that it ruins possible outlets and needed recreation.

Quite often, **the little finger** leans toward the ring finger and this means that the person is a little more persuasive than the average. This ability can be, and often is, used to console other people. Such a curve in the little finger has been called the sign of a doctor's "bedside manner." If the curve is extreme, watch out for a dynamo who could sell furnaces in the tropics. This curve also means an optimistic personality. The person believes strongly in the things he has accepted and is able to communicate his beliefs to others.

The "twisted" finger. Once in a while you will find that a finger appears to rotate to one side or to be turned on its axis. If this is not caused by an accident or injury, it shows an unusual twist to the qualities represented by the finger. The fingers' meanings are detailed in chapter thirteen.

THE FINGERS' CURVES

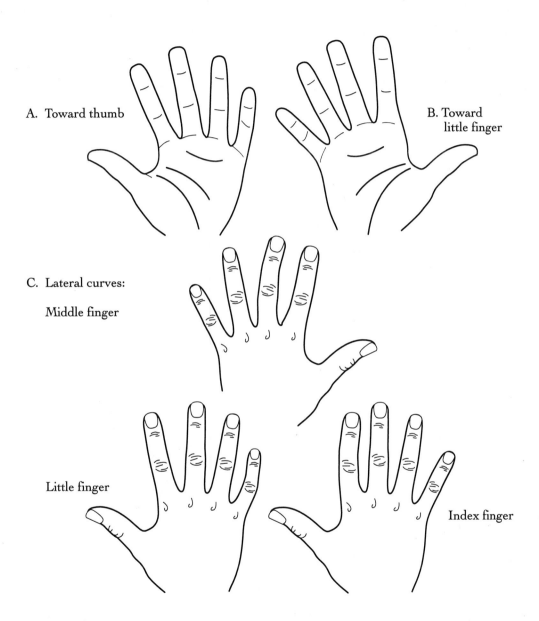

A. Toward thumb

B. Toward
   little finger

C. Lateral curves:

Middle finger

Little finger

Index finger

9

Divisions and Quadrants

*K*nowledge of the divisions and quadrants of the hand is essential for a good analysis. To be able to analyze what you are seeing in a hand, it is necessary to be able to "take the hand apart" and view it in pieces, each piece with its own meaning, and then to put it back together again, the whole enriched by the interplay of the parts.

DIVISIONS

"Divisions" of the hand refers to the three zones formed by drawing a line horizontally across the palm at the point where the thumb joins the hand, and another at the point where the fingers join the hand (Diagram A, p. 59).

The basic divisions, called "zones," help you to understand quickly just what it is that you are seeing in the palm, for the divisions, once learned, form a very useful background for relating the separate pieces of information contained throughout the hand.

With the zones, a theory that is used in other studies of man applies very nicely to the hand. This concept, which is a direct expression of man's need to structure reality into various categories of functions, involves the age-old notion of a heaven, an earth, and a hell. These categories have their parallel in the psychological terms "superego," "ego," and "id." These divisions can be applied to the hand, and in palmistry, they also are known as instinctual energy (id), social energy (ego), and mental energy (superego). Even though the labels are slightly different, the idea behind either set of terms is the same. If it helps to think of the zones in psychological terms, that is a good way to proceed; otherwise, the meanings of instinctual, social, and mental energy work nicely in relation to the palm.

The **instinctual energy zone** of the hand represents all the deeper biological drives of a person, the source of energy that must be generated and maintained to carry out all the tasks represented by the other two zones, in addition to its own function. In this sense, the zone of instinctual energy can be compared to the roots of a tree.

The **social energy zone** of the hand involves all the resources available for carrying out all aspects of the act of relating to family and society. The more prominent this zone, the more aware and involved with humanitarian interests the subject is likely to be. A person with an emphasis on this section of the hand will be found working with a number of people; much of this service will have an impersonal basis, being founded on certain ideals within the person's own mind. A prominent social energy zone suggests a definite capacity for dealing with groups of people and for perceiving deeply all the shades of meaning in human relationships. It is the people-oriented area of the hand. It also implies adaptation on the part of the subject and refers directly to the operation of the ego. Bulges in this section of the hand indicate that this is an ego not built of idle energy, that purpose is important as a guide to activity, and that the person needs activity to be happy. Certain bulges in this area point to powers of projection, to ambition, and to the ability to reach goals. However, the primary indication of such bulges is a greater degree of awareness of the world around the self.

The mental energy zone. Fingers make up the mental section of the hand. This label refers to the mind in a broad sense and embraces spiritual values, conscience, and powers of rationalization. If the fingers are quite long, then this zone is emphasized, as are the thought processes, powers of analysis, and the desire for control over the flow of life. Long fingers indicate a desire to control the process of living and usually denote an idealistic turn of mind. Short fingers do not mean that the person is not idealistic, but rather that one of the other forms of energy predominates.

Overall, **a prominent instinctual energy zone** tells you that whatever the subject does, he or she does with a great deal of personal strength and resources, with vitality and extraordinary energy. The rest of the hand will tell how this energy is channeled.

A **prominent middle zone** tells succinctly of a person who is very involved with other people, with the sharing and communicating of ideas, and, in some cases, of a person with a lively will to take whatever good things life can offer. It is a sign indicating ambition, pointing to a person who is involved with rather than detached from his or her surroundings.

Finally, a very **prominent mental energy zone**—that is, long fingers or unusually shaped fingertips—will show a person who is often preoccupied with ideas and concepts behind the facts, a person who is sensitive, aware of others' feelings, and a person who puts a very high value on loyalty.

QUADRANTS

The quadrants are especially useful as a further dimension of significance for the whole hand. These sectors concern four functions of the mind and nervous system: **conscious, unconscious, active, and passive.**

Active-passive. A horizontal line (Diagram B, p. 59) divides the palm in two at the point where the thumb is joined to the hand and stretches on across to form the active and passive zones. The reason for the labels is clear when we stop to realize that the fingers do all the "active" tasks, the motor functions commanded by the brain, and that the fingers are attached to the top of the hand, which also participates in the motions of the fingers. As for the base of the hand and its label as "passive," just think of resting the heels of your hands on a table. The hand is quiet then.

Conscious-unconscious. The last two quadrants are delineated by a vertical line drawn down the middle of the second finger (Diagram C, p. 59). Just to think a moment of the thumb and index functions makes it clearly evident why this area is labeled "conscious." As for the unconscious side, especially in the case of the ring and little fingers where the unconscious coincides with the active zone, it is as active in its own way as the conscious side. Try to pick up a rubber band or a small object from a tabletop and feel how easily the thumb and index fingers work; then note the action of the ring and little fingers together. They too work more easily than the middle and ring fingers in picking up the object. This is because the little finger has an autonomy all its own, and it plays an important role in the psyche's nonverbal expression, as the section on fingers will show (p. 81).

There are four quadrants, then, each with a hyphenated or combined meaning (Diagram D). The thumb and index finger, along with one-half of the middle finger, in the upper part of the hand, is the active-conscious quadrant; the rest of the middle, ring, and little fingers comprise the active-unconscious; the ball of the thumb to the midpoint of the hand, and down to the bottom of the hand is the conscious-passive sector; and the bottom outer edge of the hand is the unconscious-passive.

These sectors are easier to grasp once the mounts and their meanings are learned, and knowing these divisions illuminates the meanings of the mounts.

Try to relate the conscious and unconscious sectors to the active and passive areas of the hand for the easiest understanding of what they do. The conscious-passive part of the hand is more connected with expression and acting out of inner desires than the unconscious-passive, which is the storehouse of memories and dreams that, in their turn, are expressed symbolically and creatively through the arts, for instance, rather than directly or as a part of daily life. The influence of either quadrant is as strong as the mounts are high, but the strength of each area is relayed in a different manner.

These divisions may seem somewhat abstract at this point, but using them in defining the mounts will help you see how they clarify the information contained in each section of the hand.

DIVISIONS AND QUADRANTS

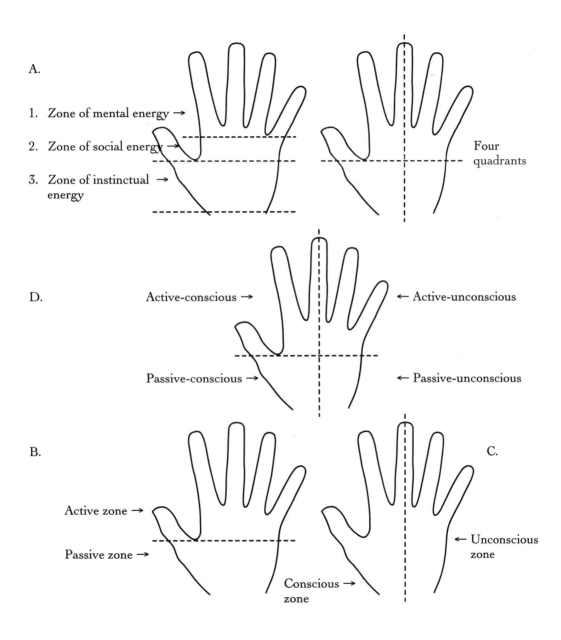

A.

1. Zone of mental energy →
2. Zone of social energy →
3. Zone of instinctual → energy

Four quadrants

D.

Active-conscious → ← Active-unconscious

Passive-conscious → ← Passive-unconscious

B.

Active zone →

Passive zone →

Conscious → zone

C.

← Unconscious zone

10

Shape and Formation
of the Palm

*U*ltimately, the shape and formation of the palm becomes a very important factor in the analysis of the temperament, personal needs, and reactions of your client. The temperament of an individual is seen especially in the formation of the palm, and the type of energy a person has is indicated by the thickness of the palm. For this reason, it is really important to note both the shape—square, spatulate, round, oblong—of the palm and its formation—its thickness.

SHAPE

People with square hands will have entirely different preoccupations and interests than people with spatulate hands, and while these two types are widely divergent, the remaining shape, the round hand, suggests yet another personality type. An oblong-palm type shares some of the interests and motivation, of the square-hand type, but is less adaptable.

The square palm (Diagram A, p. 68) belongs to a person who values productivity and craves predictable results. Concrete results speak to this person. This palm shape carries with it the great advantage of the ability to make the most of what is learned. The square-hand type is said to be "conventional," "hard working," with a love of the "tried and true." All of these generalizations apply to this shape in greater or lesser degree, but what the square shape really represents is a vital capacity to understand what is necessary in life, to adapt to things that cannot be changed. Thus, along the way, those with square palms do indeed appear to accept the conventional. How much deviation from the conventional is possible with this type of hand is determined from other signs in the palm.

When, as a palmist, you encounter palms with truly square shapes, the first thing to note is that you have come upon a person who has the ability to cope and that, even though this person has great problems, he or she can see their way through with patience and the ability to jump back from adverse circumstances. Square-handed people are loyal and dependable as a rule, and could be cited as possessing the most level-headed and enduring of temperaments. Although they are practical, however, their responses are not mechanical, for the square-handed person is blessed with foresight and a down-to-earth capacity to determine what is most beneficial and suitable for their own personal circumstances. The energy this person possesses is most often distributed and applied very well, in a balanced manner.

Spatulate palms. When the palm has a spatulate or flared shape, the energy is quite different, as are the responses to the environment. While the square-hand type loves the predictable and acts accordingly, the spatulate-handed loves just the opposite: the unpredictable, the new, the never-before experienced. Love of adventure is the keynote of the temperament. To determine whether adventure takes place mentally or is acted out, you have only to notice which end of the hand is the widest (Diagram B, p. 68).

Broad-based spatulate. When the hand is wider at the bottom, the person finds it very hard to sit still. Activity beckons at every opportunity, and the more unusual the plans are, the better. Wide-bottomed hands belong to the explorer or the person who is determined to make the most of every opportunity that presents itself. They belong to those who have healthy appetites and physical stamina. People with these hands are not easily restrained from doing whatever their curiosity and sense of adventure strongly urge them to do. They make enjoyable friends, since they are so vital, so eager to appreciate new experiences.

Broad-topped spatulate. Diagram B also shows the other type of spatulate hand. The broad edge at the top of the hand, where the fingers join the hand, speaks of a mentally restless person. Other signs in the hand will have to offer proof of an ability to carry out all the ideas this person will generate. If the symmetrical pattern of the zones of the hand is applied, the broadening at the top of the hand indicates that the desire for activity is more in the mental than in the physical realm. While a broad base to the palm shows enormous physical energy and a desire to be on the move, the same formation at the top of the hand belongs more to a visionary who might not exercise his or her natural ability as a thinker were they forced to be on the move constantly. However, those with broad-topped palms will love to hear and read about adventures, and to share them vicariously. They will no doubt have several foreign or unusual friends who satisfy their need for the unusual.

Occasionally, a person with a wide-topped palm will become quarrelsome or irritable if he or she does not channel all the mental energy they have into constructive creation. The imagination could become a vehicle of bad humor and criticism, for even though the desire for adventure does not take as physical a form as in the case of a person with a broad-based spatulate palm, the desire for activity is still greater than the average. Harnessed properly, the energy of a wide-topped hand produces a strong intellect and makes unusual achievement quite possible.

A contrast between the two types of spatulate palms could be summed up this way: broad-bottomed hands are found on persons who would rather discover new ways to climb Mt. Everest, or perhaps seek out and discover by themselves the best areas for camping, the ones with new and interesting sights, where they could entertain their friends. Meanwhile, the broad-topped type is busy entertaining his or her friends with the newest stories in town, or with the latest theories on just about any subject. The lasting preoccupation of both types, however, can be summed up as entertainment and discovery. There is no lack of excitement with either of these types, for they thrive on the unusual and will extend themselves to attain it.

There is a great deal of stamina in individuals with spatulate palms, and the projection of it is either predominantly physical or mental, depending on which area of the hand is the widest.

Round palms. "Alert" and "responsive," "fun-loving" and "lively" are the adjectives that describe the sociable people who have round palms (Diagram C, p. 68).

These people are likely to love music and any of the performing arts, anything that allows a degree of communication with the feelings of other persons. The whole range of human emotions interests these people, and they want to share what they have and experience. "Sociable" is the best way to describe their temperament, for they are most at home giving parties, imparting a joy and interest in life, and generally making those they know feel cheerful or content. Such warmth, taken to extreme, could develop into a nature that is too trusting a nature, or the possibility of spreading interests over too wide an area. The love of structure found in square hands doesn't pertain to the round hand. Neither does the love of and craving for adventure found in spatulate hands.

The oblong palm, a palm that is much longer than it is wide, is considered somewhat unusual (Diagram D, p. 68). Some sources have related this unusualness to the observation that monkeys' palms are long and have assumed that the oblong palm is an atavistic sign. There is a more reasonable explanation in terms of the zones of the hand. When a hand is as broad as it is long, then the energy represented in the bottom and top halves of the hand is easily dealt with by the conscious and unconscious zones because the zones are proportionate.

In the case of the oblong palm, the conscious and unconscious portions of the hand are shrunken and not as wide in comparison with the active and passive sectors. This disproportion helps to explain why the traditional reading of maladjustment and long, drawn-out internalization of experience is rather accurate, for one vital source of energy is not met by the balanced control inherent in a width that matches length.

Studies have shown that a long palm belongs to a very sensitive person. This sensitivity really stems from a different balance of energies, a slight tipping of the scales that makes the person feel as if he or she can't cope spontaneously or as readily as a person with a broad palm. The effect of experience is magnified because experience is not easily or smoothly assimilated. This sensitivity and slowing down in reaction can point to a very creative individual. Very often, unusual responses and perceptions are associated with this type of hand, and an artistic nature is not too uncommon a result. It can be taken for granted, in the case of those with oblong palms, that they will long remember what was said by others and the way in which it was said. Retention of experience does seem to be the norm with this type of palm, and only in conjunction with other signs, especially the mount development, is it possible to see how this retention is employed in everyday life. The fact is, this person will have to work harder to make the most of his or her potential.

A palm that is very much broader than it is long is sometimes encountered, usually accompanied by spatulate nails. This hand, needless to say, indicates a dynamo of energy. Accompanied by other signs in the palm indicating the control and direction of energy and the ability to formulate goals, it truly tells of a person who can accomplish feats out of the ordinary. Broad palms are found in people who are exuberant, loving of life, and eager to project themselves into some field of activity.

FORMATION: THICKNESS, THINNESS

The last aspect of the formation of the palm to note is the thickness or thinness of the hand. A thick hand is easily recognized for what it is, and a thin hand is also easy to spot. But, if there are doubts about whether or not a hand is thin, it is sometimes helpful to look at the center of the palm while the fingers are stretched out straight. If tendons stand out there and are readily visible, the hand is thin. This sign is also known as a "hollow palm."

Thick hands. The thicker the palm, the greater the physical stamina, and this palm belongs to persons who love to be active, who have a greater store of energy than people whose hands are thin.

Firmness and softness. When you are checking the hand for thickness, note too just how firm or soft the hand is. Softness decreases the amount of energy indicated, while firmness increases it, so that when you look at a thick hand, you know you are dealing with a person who has very great vitality if the hand is firm to the touch. A soft but thick hand shows a basic weakness or lack of desire for activity that prevents the maximum vitality in the thick hand from being used. If a hand is thick and quite hard and unbending, then the client does not easily listen to others or adapt to new conditions that require him or her to form a new outlook. The ideal hand is firm without being too hard or too soft.

Thin hands. When you examine a thin hand, you know that this person has great sensitivity and is probably very refined. He or she may have a broad range of feeling, but, for the most part, it is kept inside rather than projected. A soft hand in this instance can well mean laziness, but it is hard to determine if the soft or "lazy" quality is a result of the lower energy level shown in the thin hand, or if a lack of activity is the most convenient way to adjust. A firm but thin hand indicates the advantage of the ability to make good use of the energy that is available, even though that energy is less than in the case of thicker hands. Positively viewed, thin hands mark a very refined person, one who is more apt to be intellectual in their approach or dreamy in their projections in everyday life. People with thin hands make good researchers or clerical help. They also make lively dinner or party guests when a stimulating level of conversation is called for.

In summary, a thick hand signals great energy, drive, and an active nature; a thin hand shows sensitivity, some innate reticence that is usually expressed as refinement, and a tendency to be very alert mentally, with an active and questioning mind. The emphasis on mind versus body is directly related to the proportionate thinness or thickness of the hand. A thin hand shows a person who is cerebral in orientation and a thick hand points to a person who thrives on physical activity of all sorts.

"Hollow" palms have had a bad connotation in some past theories of palmistry, but it never automatically follows that people who have these hollow palms, palms with a depressed center and visible tendons, will experience misfortune. Many times the misfortunes associated with this palm are nothing but the person's reactions to events, for with this type of palm the skin is indeed thin. The old reference to being "thin-skinned" has an almost literal application here.

There are cases where individuals learn to adjust to their own sensitivity and can turn finely tuned perceptions into a means of relating extraordinarily well to others. It isn't uncommon to find successful lecturers or people involved with group work who have hollow palms, which are a sign of the energy expended.

A corollary seems to follow from this observation. The fact that so many times people whose palms are hollow are found working in group projects and humanitarian endeavors points to an unusually large expenditure of time and energy. What these persons channel into relating with many types of people (because their sensitivity and perception make this possible) becomes energy lost to them for their own purposes. The only caution for people with these "hollow" palms is that they must be sure to monitor their activities and outpouring of attention to others so that they have enough energy left to plan their own lives efficiently.

The actual shape of the palm is the structure that tells how individuals will react to their environment: with order and caution as the square-hand type does, with the flair and aggressiveness of the spatulate-handed, with the amiability and love of people seen in the round-palmed, or with the unusual insight and timing of those with oblong palms. Thickness or lack of it adds further confirmation of just how much energy the person has and how he or she is prepared to use it.

HAND SHAPES

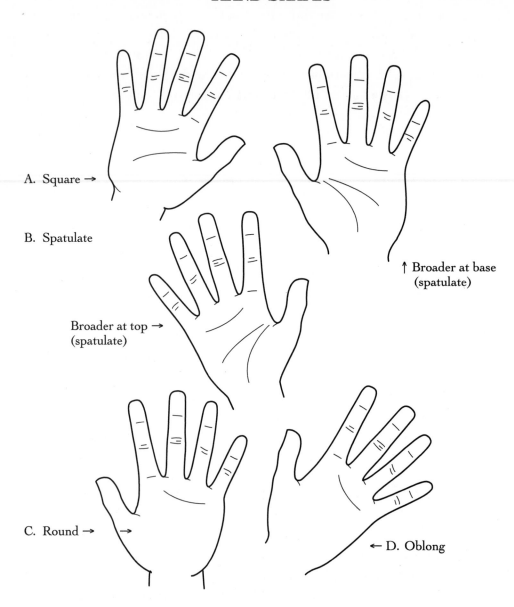

A. Square →

B. Spatulate

↑ Broader at base
(spatulate)

Broader at top →
(spatulate)

C. Round →

← D. Oblong

11

Fingertips

So much of palmistry has to do with the shapes of the hands and fingers that the ability to recognize and identify the various shapes is a real asset. Acquiring this ability takes some practice, especially in working with the fingertips.

Here is where immediate application of shape is important to the reading. As you read a hand you are very aware of the shapes you are seeing—they register almost unconsciously—and this awareness helps to define what you are seeing.

According to ancient palmistry lore, the fingertips had great significance, for it was their shape alone that determined how energy entered and circulated throughout the body. The notion that special energy—life itself, in fact—entered through the fingertips came about when the ancients noted that a baby drawing its first breath invariably held its fingertips straight and rigid, for the hands were jerked open as the baby took in air.

Following this point, let's suppose for a moment that life and energy do enter the body for the first time through the fingertips. Then the shape of the fingertips will have a bearing on how the energy enters, for this life-force, it is assumed, will have to accommodate itself to the physical shapes in order to get into the body.

There are four basic shapes to the fingertips: tapered, round, square, and flared (Diagram A, p. 73). These shapes in palmistry are also known as "psychic," "conic," "square," and "spatulate."

With tapered tips, energy entering the body has to resist very little bulk. Round or conic tips offer a little more resistance to the energy's entrance, while square tips present even more of a barrier, and flared tips form a veritable obstacle. Resistance to energy is proportionate to expanding width in the fingertips.

Some of the qualities the energy had to assume in order to "break into" the body linger in the personality: placidness and gentleness (slimmer fingertips), sturdiness and utility (square tips), and strong, constant activity (flared tips).

Specific personality traits have become associated with each shape. Because **a pointed fingertip** lets in energy more rapidly, in a swift motion, it represents a mind that works rapidly, absorbing impressions at times without being conscious of doing so. **The round-tipped finger** shows a mind that works smoothly, without friction. To enter **square tips,** energy has to slow down, and so these tips show a mind fond of working with details, patient and constructive in many ways. Given that the flared tip creates a big barrier to energy's entrance, the energy has to double its effort to enter the tip, and, in doing this, it sets up reverberating waves of excitement and agitation. Thus the lively temperament of a flared-fingertip personality is set in motion.

Let's take a closer look at the traits associated with each fingertip shape.

Even though **square fingertips** show a love of detail, this doesn't necessarily mean that the person will like to work with details; he or she may simply appreciate others who do. The mentality associated with these tips is an analytical one that seeks to get inside a situation by becoming familiar with all its sides or parts. This analytical turn of mind will be applied especially to areas that interest these people. If a square-fingertip personality loves math, then the person will be interested in dissecting mathematical theories just to have a better appreciation of how the whole functions. If the person loves watchmaking or model airplane building, he or she will enjoy taking apart the object and will put it together with much attention paid to detail.

The painstaking outlook is applied to reasoning and craftsmanship with equal ease. A plastic surgeon would do well to have square-tipped fingers, for his or her patients could be confident of the quality of the work—exhibiting attention to details combined with an appreciation of overall appearance.

Here it is a good idea to point out that fingertip shapes do not guarantee the field of activity that people will choose, although there is a correlation between temperament and vocation. No one field or type of job is ever filled with just one personality type. Fingertip shape is a guide to what type of job would suit the person best. Personal flexibility and circumstances that the person has no control over may dictate a certain kind of work be done. Then the skills a person has must find their application wherever possible within the framework of the job.

A plastic surgeon with round fingertips would have the love of beauty associated with this fingertip, but not the same technical skill as a surgeon with square fingertips, but determination to learn can make up the difference.

Those with round fingertips always need beauty and harmonious surroundings for maximum development of individual potential. Those with flared tips, however, seem to thrive under stress and challenge. Those with gentler, round-tipped fingers need tranquillity to flourish. They love people-oriented activities. They do well in any job where beauty and harmony are the end products. They make good beauticians, care well for pets, and often work with music or art. A sense of balance is important to them.

Flared or spatulate tips denote a need for exercise. That can be putting it politely, for the restlessness of this type can wear out less-active souls. A very striking example of the yen for adventure and the unusual can be seen in the photograph of one flared-fingertip explorer who was photographed writing in a notebook while resting in the jaws of a newly dead crocodile. Energetic personalities like these strive for the unusual, and their impulses have to have an outlet, or everyone in the vicinity will be miserable. These people have inquiring minds that will not accept conventional answers. They make good teachers, for they awaken perceptions in those they teach.

Determining the shape of fingertips is sometimes thought to be difficult. One of the best aids in this determination is to feel the fingertip, running your own fingers down the sides of the tip and up again. In this way, you can feel the amount of resistance offered. This type of test is most useful in cases where confusion arises over the questions "Is it square or round?" or "Is it square or flared?" Round tips offer less resistance to touch than square tips and flared tips offer the most resistance of all.

Pointed fingertips are so distinct in shape that there is little question of what one is viewing in their case. These tips are often found on entertainers, people in the arts who make use of their feelings and intuitions to communicate well.

It is no coincidence that much of Hollywood seems to be enamored of psychics. There is a common bond between the natures of a performer and a psychic, natures that are rooted in the need to communicate and usually aided by an unusual degree of perceptive feeling. Pointed fingers also show an approach to everyday life that is perhaps eccentric or whimsical and a result of a need to be different. Self-expression is very important to people with tips like these, for they are creative dreamers. They could also be successful in advertising, for they have an intuitive awareness of what pleases. Their ideas are ahead of the times. Painting or poetry can be very good outlets for their feelings. Exactly what medium of self-expression is needed can be determined by other signs in the hands.

Variations in fingertip shape. If all the fingers have but one shape, the person is considered a pure type and the qualities associated with the shape will be easily discerned. More often than not, a variety of shapes will exist on the fingertips. In this case, the analysis will have to be made on an individual basis. Each finger represents something different and the shape will point to the person's approach to the areas represented by the finger.

FINGERTIP SHAPES

A. Fingertip shapes

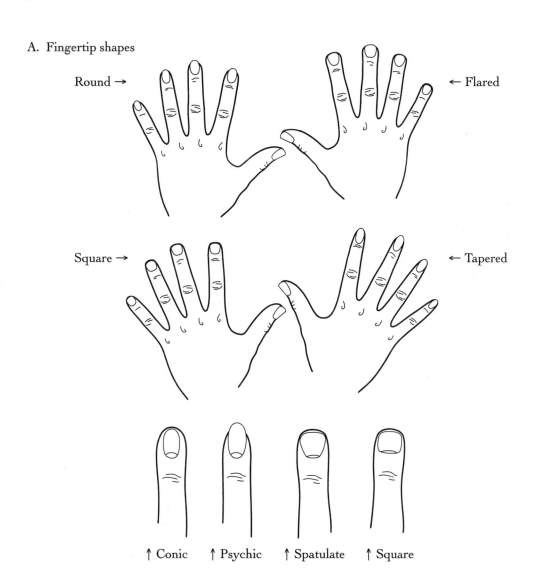

Round →

← Flared

Square →

← Tapered

↑ Conic   ↑ Psychic   ↑ Spatulate   ↑ Square

12

**Finger Length
and Meaning**

In palmistry, finger length is an important clue to the way a person deals with situations he or she encounters, whether at work or at home. The longer the fingers are, the greater the attention to detail, the more of a perfectionist the person is likely to be. Short fingers do not mean, though, that a person is careless. Short fingers belong to personalities who thrive on diversity. These people are lively and like to spread their time and talents out into more than one area. There is a quickness of mind associated with short fingers and an ability to see the entire picture without having all the details spelled out.

THE LENGTH OF THE FINGERS AS A WHOLE

There is one and only one way to measure the length of the fingers, and that is to measure them against the palm to which they belong! Many times you may have heard it said, "What long fingers you have!" when in reality what is long is the palm itself. A long palm gives the impression of long fingers, and usually a long palm is just what makes the fingers short by comparison. This is a vital point, for there is a world of difference between the temperaments and needs associated with long and short fingers.

To measure the length of all the fingers, taken as a whole, all that is necessary is to use the middle finger as the gauge or "spokesperson" for the group by measuring its length and transferring this same length to the palm for comparison. A ruler or centimeter measure can be used to record the length of the middle finger and then it can be placed along the palm.

The average finger length is a mark that takes up seven-eighths of the palm. Anything longer—fingers that are as long as the palm itself, for instance—are defined as "long," and anything under the seven-eighths mark is "short."

Should the fingers be exactly seven-eighths of the palm in length, the signs attributed to long and short fingers will have to be verified elsewhere in the palm.

If seven-eighths of the palm is a hard measurement to visualize, it helps to divide the palm into eight equal sections and count seven down from the top of the palm. Once you see this point and can visualize it on your own hand, it is easy enough to gauge on other hands.

Short fingers are found on people who tend to be enthusiastic about new projects or issues that interest them, but who don't like to be involved in a tedious or lengthy working out of ideas. Their method of problem solving is to go straight to the central issue and, for this reason, these people can be blunt. If their enthusiasm is stimulated, they are charming and outgoing, warm and energetic. Their attention is always centered on the heart of what interests them, and so they are dynamic and often good at investigative techniques. Journalists and detectives, experts at the managerial level, and nearly every intuitive thinker ideally will have short fingers, if indeed they have the ability to pare away nonessentials and get down to business.

Long fingers show a tendency to stray from the central issue, to get wrapped up in details. Such people are most at home with particulars rather than generalities. Long fingers show a sensitive nature, one that is slower in responding to all that is perceived, but in the long run, more thorough. The difference between long and short fingers is well-illustrated by the story of the tortoise and the hare—except that the ending varies, and no conclusion can be drawn as to which tendency is the best to have.

Long-fingered people frequently are idealistic about their friends and people dear to them, and loyalty is important to them. These qualities are what they look for in friends and what they themselves are prepared to give.

In certain paintings, especially in those of El Greco, long fingers—and hands—are often used to denote an attitude of spirituality or high aspiration. This is accurate from the point of view of palmistry. Very long fingers are found on people who are contemplative and not very fond of activity for its own sake. These traits are in direct contrast to those possessed by short-fingered people, who find it very hard to sit still. Put very simply, as a guideline for easy reference rather than as an absolute conclusion, long fingers belong to the thinkers and short fingers to the doers.

THE LENGTH OF INDIVIDUAL FINGERS

Each finger, including the thumb, which is usually treated separately from the other fingers, has its own ideal length. The thumb, for instance, is expected to extend up to one-half of the bottom section of the index finger (Diagram A, p. 90). Meanings for the thumb will be given along with traits for the rest of the fingers.

Thickness and thinness. To analyze the fingers well, the length of each finger has to be considered, as does its thick or thin appearance. Thick fingers show several traits that are best summed up as a heightened appetite for life and sensual pleasures. As a result of this heightened appetite and interest in life, the perceptions are swift and intuitive. Thin fingers show a personality interested in lofty ideals and aesthetics and possessing a strong sense of economy. People with thin fingers often are reluctant to speak their minds freely, either because they do not wish to hurt others' feelings or because of a strong sense of propriety and respect for the other person.

When the fingers are measured individually, there is a definite ratio considered to be ideal: both the index and the ring fingers should be half a tip shorter than the middle finger; and the little finger should reach exactly to the line dividing the top section of the ring finger from the middle section.

The three sections. Each finger is composed of three sections, sometimes known as phalanges, and each section has its own significance. In Diagram B (p. 90), the sections are labeled 1, 2, and 3. The first sections represent the intellect and intuition; the second section, the ability to organize and relate facts, an appreciation of structure; and the third sections, physical vigor and an appreciation of earthy things. People who literally feel close to the earth or who work in occupations connected with it often have these long third sections.

In a sense, in a descending order from one to three, each section is increasingly associated with physical realities. The first sections have no connection with the tangible and concrete other than as they symbolize the process by which all that has been experienced in the physical and concrete realms is absorbed by the mind. The middle sections are the links between nonphysical and physical experience, and as such are indicative of the process of relating what is learned to what has already been experienced. The third section symbolizes the realm of physical experience itself.

The way these three sections work should be applied to the fingers' meanings. Knowing the emphasis indicated by each section of the fingers—intellectual, rational, or physical—you can analyze the meaning of the finger according to the predominant tendency shown in the sections. This tendency can be inferred on the basis of the thickness of the sections and their relative length. The analysis of the thumb at the end of the chapter demonstrates how to interpret the sections.

The first step in learning about the fingers is to give them a name. Traditionally, in palmistry all the fingers except the thumb have been called by astrological names. Originally, this occurred because the fingers were closely associated with the mounts directly underneath them and shared in the names. The reason for astrological names for mounts was a good one, as we shall see in the chapter on the mounts, but today, if it feels better to give the fingers names that are not astrological, it is perfectly acceptable. In this case, the fingers are usually referred to as the first (index), second, third, and fourth—just as they are called in common parlance.

The astrological terms for the fingers are:

- **Index:** Jupiter
- **Middle:** Saturn
- **Ring:** Apollo
- **Little:** Mercury

THE JUPITER FINGER

Stop and think how you use your Jupiter finger. Don't you often point with it to express or emphasize your ideas or use it as a shorthand signal in asking another person to do something for you? Such usage underlines the principal function of the index finger as a reflector of authority. From this meaning we get a reading of leadership, admiration for authority and higher institutions, strong religious feelings, protective and paternal or maternal feelings, teaching and guidance.

Think of someone making a dramatic point or someone eager to communicate something she or he feels is important, and you will get a picture of someone pausing with an index finger poised straight up in the air, as if the person were saying, "Just a minute!" The Jupiter finger is used to indicate a flow of thought or to stem another flow of thought. In a good Jupiter finger we see powers of concentration and a capacity for undivided attention.

A person who uses the index finger to point usually is a person preoccupied with clear communication and with getting his or her point across. Such a gesture is emphatic.

In all cases where there is knowledge or communication, there is a source. The source becomes authority, and authority in its turn has duties. Protection and guidance are the principal duties and, stemming from this, a natural love of children and animals.

There is one other function of the index finger to consider: a baby first traces his or her mother's face with an index finger. As the baby feels the outline of the mother's face, she or he receives the first impression of something outside the self. Later, the index finger will always be the first to explore objects that arouse curiosity. This exploratory gesture is symbolic and, at the same time, a physical expression of a very important function of the Jupiter finger: to represent our perception of reality.

The bent Jupiter finger. As long as the finger is not unusual or curved in any way, the perception of reality follows normal courses, but with any unusual configuration to the finger, you will be alerted that the client does not perceive things in quite the way that others do. The person may feel somewhat of a misfit and consequently inferior, or may be very proud of her or his individuality. When the finger curves laterally, there is an involuntary announcement, just as drooping shoulders can signal fatigue. The curved index finger (Diagram C, p. 90) says that the client recoils from ordinary interaction with outside events. This is precisely why it is the mark of an individualist.

Average length. The Jupiter finger should stand straight and be average in length. This means that your client is able to work well with others and, in general, is successful in personal relationships.

The long Jupiter finger. If this finger is very long, nearly as long as the middle finger, then the person needs to be a leader. There is a capacity for domination, and your client finds it easy to take charge of situations. These qualities take a certain amount of courage, and self-confidence is always a trait associated with a long Jupiter finger.

The short Jupiter finger. If the finger falls short of its average length (Diagram D, p. 91), a half-tip shorter than the middle finger, the person will be reticent and many times unable to exert the control he or she wishes over their environment. This happens mainly because the person is open to too many impressions and stimuli, can be swayed by what is seen, and finds it hard to organize what is perceived. There can be a continuous feeling of weakness and a lack of ego. One person with a short index finger once commented: "I barely have sufficient ego to cope with the mundane world."

On the plus side, such a person will be very considerate of others' feelings, for he or she doesn't want to intrude, ever. This person is innately modest, but would do well to increase a positive self-image, and to dwell on his or her strengths. If your client has a short index finger, you will have to convince him or her to believe more in themselves and their own powers and to refuse to rely on others. Their low self-concept can make them choose friends indiscriminately or unwisely, since they don't have a sense of control or self-worth that will let them express themselves on a par with people they consider superior. The solution is to narrow the gap between the self-worth they think they have and the power they imagine others have.

Extreme length. An index finger that is quite long, as long as the middle finger itself, suggests traits of bossiness or indomitability. There will, however, be nothing willy-nilly or wishy-washy about what this person does. If this person can tone down a tendency to plan and direct without benefit of input from others and will take the time to explain why they wish to put a certain plan into action, then everyone can profit from their talents. This person is guided by faith and confidence in his or her own inner powers and has a strong sense of direction in life.

THE SATURN FINGER

Another type of inner power and sense of direction can be found in the middle or Saturn finger. This finger is very interesting just by virtue of its position. In chapter nine, page 55, we saw that a vertical line is drawn down the middle of this finger to define the conscious and unconscious zones of the hand.

Saturn's main role in the hand is integrative. Both the conscious and unconscious drives meet and come to focus in this finger. Because it is a borderline zone of two of the most important functions of the hand, this finger takes on special importance. It becomes a symbolic point of balance.

Average length. A sense of inner equilibrium and propriety shows itself through this finger. If the length is average (Diagram E, p. 91)—half a tip longer than the index and ring fingers—just enough sense of balance, discipline, and self-control are indicated. If the finger is long, these qualities become exaggerated and take the form of inhibition or an overly serious outlook.

A long middle finger always signals a strong sense of duty and responsibility. This can be channeled in a good way, however, and produce a very well-balanced and thoughtful person, as long as the tendency to take things too seriously is controlled. What often accompanies the strong sense of the propriety of things, if other signs don't balance the serious temperament associated with a long middle finger, is a capacity for guilt and worry.

If your client has a long middle finger, you will know that a sense of duty, a tendency to worry, and the habit of holding things inside are present, but you will also find that this person thinks very deep thoughts.

When the middle finger is long, then the "stage" or field of action for the integration of conscious and unconscious forces is large, and the two forces become actors with a lot of latitude for demonstrating their powers. Persons who have such a "stage" built into their hands have been the captive audience of long and noisy scenes between the conscious and unconscious minds. These individuals have retained some of the inner dialogue that is foisted upon them by the two "actor" forces. This is why your clients will have deep and unusual perceptions to convey. This unique position of the Saturn or middle finger and the stage it provides for the interaction of conscious and unconscious forces explains the traditional interpretation of "gloom" and "inhibition" for a long finger. A long finger reflects a less automatic or superficial acceptance of everyday events.

A short Saturn finger doesn't mean that the conscious and unconscious forces are quiet—not at all. These forces are always active in the psyche, and the finger still remains the dividing line between these two zones, but when the finger is short, the stage for interaction between the two zones is eclipsed, in a certain sense, and the forces work in the dark. Their voices are not heard so compellingly by the person with a short middle finger. So then, traditionally, this type of finger means a carefree attitude, a bohemian outlook. All this really means is that the person with a short middle finger is not overtaken by the vortex of power associated with the finger. It means that he or she is able to live out daily life apparently unhindered by preoccupations that seem to strike others.

Just as a long middle finger is more of a structure symbolically accommodating the interplay of conscious and unconscious forces, a finger of such length shows an appreciation of and need for structure to compensate for the increased sensitivity to the life of the psyche. In the same way, just as the short middle finger is less of a structure, those who possess it have less need for structure in their daily lives. Since a person with a short middle finger doesn't need even the normal amount of structure indicated by a middle finger of average length, much less the great amount of structure suggested by the long finger, this person certainly will look carefree and bohemian by comparison.

THE APOLLO FINGER

If the bohemian outlook indicated by a short middle finger promises a certain joy, then yet another type of joy and contentment will be signaled by the ring finger. This finger is the first finger to lie entirely in the unconscious zone of the hand.

Average length. If this finger is of average length—that is, one-half tip shorter than the middle finger—the unconscious forces are shown to be in proportion to the conscious forces. The powers of creativity associated with the unconscious find nice expression in someone with a well-formed ring finger. When the finger is average in length, creativity flows smoothly and does not overtake or control other aspects of the person's life. Powers of creativity are enhanced when the finger stands straight and has no curves of any sort. The creativity will work along the lines indicated by the shape of the fingertip: within a well-defined structure if the tip is square; bolstered by an artistic sense and an appreciation of beauty if the tip is oval; and in an unusual and innovative way if the tip is spatulate.

The ring finger also marks powers of adjustment and adaptability. **Average length** means that the person can adapt to whatever he encounters. **A long ring finger** means that the adaptation takes the form of rationalization or a struggle to dominate the environment by projecting inner needs at such a pitch that everything encountered is subdued. **A short ring finger** means that the powers of adaptation operate by "shrinking" away from what is encountered in the environment. Both the long and short ring fingers can signal a struggle, but the long finger is more positive because the ability to project inner needs and creativity is stronger. The person with a very short ring finger simply denies or shuts off the flow of his or her dreams and inner life in order to adapt to what she or he encounters.

Traditionally, **a short ring finger** means that the person is not using all their own powers of creativity and therefore they remain frustrated. This interpretation is certainly possible, but at times the person fails to recognize the frustration, for he or she has given up and quit looking for ways to express him- or herself. If your client has a short ring finger, take time to explore signs of talent and ability in the hands. You can help point him or her in the direction of fulfillment and give them necessary support or encouragement.

THE MERCURY FINGER

Encouragement is not what will be needed by a person having a long little finger.

The length of little fingers is determined by the line that marks the tip of the ring finger. A little finger of average length just touches that line. If the little finger is actually as long as most of the tip of the ring finger, it is a very long little finger indeed. Short little fingers fall short of the line (see Diagram F, p. 91).

The little finger is traditionally the "messenger of the unconscious," and it is very active in its position at the end of the hand. There is a lot of movement independent of other fingers. Movement, in fact, is the key to this finger. The longer the finger, or the livelier its gestures, the more lively the person is likely to be.

A long little finger means excellent powers of self-expression, all coming from a quick and unconscious absorption of impressions and intuitions. The little finger indicates an efficient feedback mechanism for what is absorbed unconsciously: the more that goes in, the more that flows out. Long little fingers mean the ability to be eloquent, in speech and all gestures, and an ability to imitate others. Mimicry is only natural, for the mind has been absorbing at length all the verbal and nonverbal clues others offer, and some of this has to surface.

The short little finger. Because the little finger symbolizes a channel for the absorption of information, impressions, and perceptions, a short little finger indicates the same capacity to receive information as a long little finger. The difference between the two is that there is a lessened channel for outflow of impressions accompanying a tiny little finger. There will still be expression and acting out of what is perceived, but the expression is likely to be narrowed in some way. Thus the short little finger tells of either the ability to concentrate on specific fields of endeavor or a tendency to have diverse interests, none of which are treated in depth.

Traditionally, short little fingers are associated with bluntness, temper, or a tendency to put one's foot in one's mouth.

All of these readings make sense. Bluntness would come from the need to concentrate with intensity on a single field, a trait associated with a short little finger. Temper is a logical result of the foreshortened channel, which does not allow the person to express outwardly all that she or he has perceived. The flow of what has gone in and must come out is uneven, and this unevenness produces impatience. The tendency to put one's foot in one's mouth seems to be the traditional reading that holds up less than the others. Many people with short little fingers do not make this mistake. It would seem that this meaning originally came about as the opposite of the eloquence associated with a long little finger.

Long little fingers. There is no doubt that long little fingers mean eloquence—the ability to give back, to surface what is learned, and to give it life and expression.

Long little fingers mean that a person is exuberant, optimistic, and full of faith in a way that others aren't. These qualities are a result of the flow between what is perceived and what is expressed. There is harmony within the personality.

Very long little fingers can mean an exaggerated ability for feedback, and the outflow is so tremendous that it can get rearranged in the process. That is, what those with very long little fingers perceive comes to the surface in such a rush that the original substance and content can be altered.

If your client has these long little fingers reaching well into the area of the ring fingertip, you will find him or her clever and adept with words and perceptions. The reading will be an interesting one, for this person, with strong powers of assimilating any information, will feed right back to you what you have just said, but you will have to be quick enough to determine if there is a new element added to the meanings you intended to put across.

Long little fingers indicate success in careers where the use of words is important. Lawyers have long little fingers, as do successful salespeople.

Short little fingers sometimes reveal a sense of inferiority on the person's part, especially if the finger is set low on the hand (Diagram G, p. 91).

You can explore with your client some of the reasons for this feeling of inferiority. Because the little finger itself is associated with feelings about parents or the opposite sex, inferiority feelings often come from the same source. Knowing this, you have a starting point for dialogue.

Long little fingers. Traditionally, little fingers that are well defined and long also mean ability in science and medicine. If your client is inclined to like these areas of study, he or she would have a natural ability for them, provided other signs in the hand corroborate this natural ability. You need to know if other traits show an ability to concentrate, for example, or a flair for math and a sense of dedication. Will power in achieving any goal becomes the central issue whenever you are interpreting talent in the hand.

THE THUMB

Palmists look to the thumb for signs of will power, steadiness of purpose, application, consistency, and the ability to achieve any goal once it has been set. A good thumb will mean all of these things.

A thumb should be studied for its length, thickness, special shapes, and for its three sections. All of these elements define the thumb's meanings.

Further definition of the thumb comes from its position on the hand. This finger, along with the ball of the thumb, known as the Mount of Venus, forms a central part of the hand and enables the hand to be what it is. For this reason, the thumb is usually treated separately from the fingers. In palmistry, special attention is given to the fact that the thumb is a distinguishing feature of humans, and that its position in reference to the other fingers makes it a lever. All the other fingers work as a unit in cooperation with the thumb, which stands by itself.

The thumb has three sections, just like the other fingers, although the third section is the mount itself—in this the thumb differs from any of the other fingers, whose mounts are separate. Although the thumb contains a completely self-sufficient set of information, the analysis of it can follow the patterns used in analyzing other parts of the hand.

The sections of the thumb. Through sectional analysis, the first section, or the tip of the thumb, can be assumed to refer to the mental qualities, just as other fingertips do. The middle section then refers to powers of rationalization and of relating one set of information to another. The third section of the thumb, the Mount of Venus, indeed refers to physical sensations and preoccupations—and more. To understand this third section of the thumb, you will have to read the section on the Mount of Venus, for it embraces the physical world in all its expanded meaning. The actual life force of a person resides in the Mount of Venus, and it is appropriate that this forms the third section of the thumb.

Think of the thumb as the root of the hand itself. If this "root" is long, strong, and sturdy, then it is powerful and conveys the qualities of steadiness, will power, and dedication. A good thumb indicates a person who endures and who is not blown by the winds of changing events and circumstances.

A short thumb shows a person who is swayed by emotions, by what others say and do.

To measure the thumb's length, check it to see if, when it rests against the side of the hand, the tip comes halfway up the bottom joint of the index finger. A very long thumb will reach all the way up to the line that divides the second and third sections of the index finger. Very short thumbs reach just to the bottom of the index finger itself.

The thumb is so important that a person possessing a short one, no matter how talented she or he is, will have difficulty fulfilling the potential in their hand. All tendencies toward underachievement will have to be combatted. An awareness of the tendency to do less than she or he can will not be enough to help your client. They probably know this without having it confirmed by their thumb. As a palmist you can help by giving positive encouragement to reach higher in their aims. What they need is inspiration that will provide the drive to do the things they know they can do.

A short thumb does not mean that the person will never accomplish anything; it means he or she will have to work twice as hard to fight a natural tendency to let things go, to take the line of least resistance.

A long thumb implies a natural ability to accomplish desired goals, and it is no coincidence that men and women who are prominent or who have achieved a position of power usually have long or well-formed thumbs. If a person with a short thumb reaches a position of power, it will be due to very strong efforts on his or her part, and possibly to the aid of other people. The true test of anyone who has reached the summit is to see if he or she remains there. Those with longer thumbs have greater *natural* staying power.

Thick thumbs mean forcefulness. Such thumbs make it possible for the person to get their way, but the path will not be easy or necessarily rewarding, for obstacles are sometimes not truly conquered but simply trodden upon—momentarily.

If your client has a thick thumb—and you won't have trouble recognizing it—take time to talk over the various things he or she has achieved and how they did it.

When you are studying the thickness of the thumb, you have to analyze it in two sections: the first and the second joints of the thumb. One may be thick, or both may be thick. Each section has a special meaning.

A thick tip means extremely strong will power and stubbornness. A thin tip shows energy that gives out suddenly and less ability to stick with things when the going gets rough. However, **a thin tip** on the thumb marks a person who is tactful and who won't insist on dominating the scene. He or she simply hasn't got the resources to dominate. They need their rest, while someone with a thick tip to the thumb can keep going when others would drop from exhaustion (Diagram H, p. 92).

A thick second section (Diagram I) shows that the client doesn't like to be reasoned with. His or her mind is made up on most issues and events. There is a stubbornness that comes from having a set mind.

A good thumb can have either **a medium-thick** or **a thin second section** (Diagram J, p. 92). The medium-thick second section suggests that the powers of rationalization are kept on a par with the will power a person has. There is a balance between the two.

A thin second section has always been found on tactful people. It shows an open mind, a receptive mind, which will turn over all points of view before making any choices. If the second section is much longer than the tip (Diagram K, p. 92), the person is likely to reason and reason without acting. This has been called the "Hamlet" thumb, and the person does seem to sing the song of "to be or not to be." You can advise your client about this tendency and the need to make decisions. With effort, this person can become more decisive in his or her actions.

A thumb that is thin overall, but well defined and graceful, shows a tactful, lively person. This person appreciates different types of people and has an open mind.

Travel appeals to this person, too. His or her mind is quick, and they will probably have interesting stories to tell.

There are a few special shapes to the thumb that have their own meanings. These readings involve the tip of the thumb.

Clubbed thumbs. If the tip becomes very thick (Diagram L, p. 92), a hereditary predisposition to anger is indicated. Even if the thumb isn't seen on any members of the immediate family, chances are that someone in the past had it. This thumb has been called the "clubbed thumb" and has been associated with violent or criminal natures. This conclusion shouldn't be formed too quickly. The person may never have encountered circumstances that would have aroused a violent temper. It is good to keep in mind, though, that this person can be aroused to anger and that there is no precise way to know just what will cause the anger.

Flat thumbs. Some thumb tips look flat or depressed. This means that the person needs more physical exercise than he or she gets. There is a tendency to feel tired or to collapse after any unusual efforts. This tendency could be overcome by a regular program of physical exercise, for the body has to be kept in shape to meet any unusual drains on energy (Diagram M, p. 92).

Supple and stiff thumbs. There is another special sign found in the thumb. If the thumb is supple at the knuckle dividing the tip and second section, the thumb will bend backwards in an arc. If the knuckle isn't flexible, the thumb stays straight. These two types of thumb are called "supple" and "stiff" (Diagram N, p. 92).

The supple thumb means a generous person, one who will give freely of his or her time, money, and sympathy. This person loves a good time and loves to entertain. Very often, this thumb indicates dramatic talent. A little bend in the thumb shows a sympathetic nature, but if the arc is exaggerated, the person may be taken in by others' hard luck stories, and at all times will have difficulty holding on to their money. A supple thumb is a sure sign of a willing spender.

The stiff thumb. Budgets and control over the flow of their money are characteristic of stiff-thumb types. On the positive side, this person has the capacity for good self-control, although other signs in the hand might add or detract from this inference. A stiff thumb shows a person who is not spontaneous in responding to new situations. The tried and true is the only framework within which their comfortable creativity will be exercised. If you want to make this client feel at ease, speak of things that are familiar to her or him, and you will notice a growing relaxation that will help them open up to you.

Flexibility and resistance. As a last check, to complete your analysis of the thumb, notice again the resistance or flexibility it offers (chapter eight).

The thumb that offers resistance to your touch as you try to move it indicates a quality of control in the personality. If the thumb has the money-spending, sympathetic arc, the lack of mobility at the bottom where the thumb joins the hand will demonstrate that some of the extravagance is held in check. If the thumb is thick, indicating a stubborn set of mind, the lack of mobility will indicate an increased stubbornness. Read this resistance as control and add it to all the signs from the thumb for a complete reading.

Of all the signs seen in the thumb, the most important are its length and overall appearance. If you notice nothing else, be sure to check the length of the thumb, for it above all tells you how much the person can naturally achieve. It will help define the effort your client has to make to realize the potential reflected in his hand.

To learn quite a few of the details of your client's potential, you have to look at the mounts, for they tell the type and amount of energy an individual has.

THE THUMBS

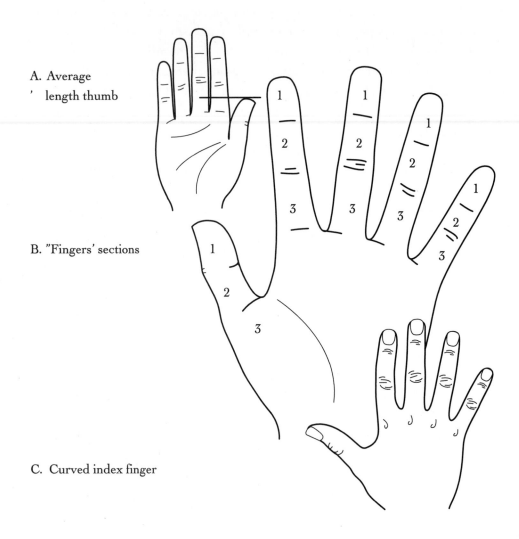

A. Average
'   length thumb

B. "Fingers' sections

C. Curved index finger

D. Jupiter finger length

Average →   Short →

E. Saturn finger length →

Average →   Long →

F. Mercury finger length

Average →

(G.) ↑

G. Mercury finger set low on hand

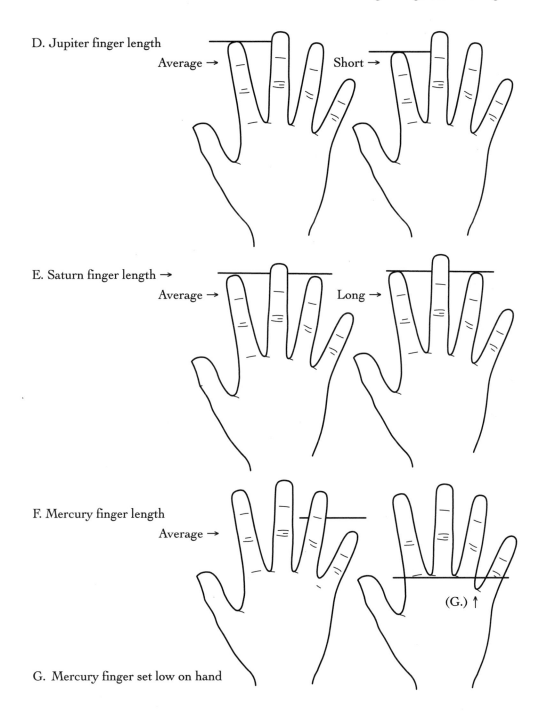

THUMB TIPS

H. Thin or thick, side view ↓

Second
sections

I. Thick ↑   J. Thin ↑

K. Long second section ↓

THUMB TYPES

L. Clubbed thumb ↓

M. Flat
thumb ↓

N. Stiff thumb, flexible thumb ↓

13

The Mounts of the Hands

*T*he mounts of the hand are all the elevated areas on the palm. These areas are ordinarily categorized as eleven defined mounts: Jupiter, Saturn, Apollo, Mercury, two mounts of Mars, the Plain of Mars, Venus, Luna, and recently, the mounts of Neptune and Pluto.

It may seem that these areas are given astrological names, but the names for astrology and for palmistry are derived from the same source: early studies of humanity that make up our mythology.

All energy is an expression of very real but often unseen forces. Early humans tamed the forces they encountered by naming them. The names were those of the gods and goddesses who were thought to embody and represent these forces, and because humans desperately wanted to relate to these forces, the gods were given human characteristics. In this whole panorama, humans had a role to play as the reflection of the forces they experienced and named. In effect, humans became a reflection of the cosmos, and then another step was taken. In further efforts to understand themselves and the powers they reflected, humans chose to decipher the hand as a reflection of their human self. Visually, the relationship between all these elements is easily seen. In the heavens, stars had five points, or at least they came to be depicted that way by humanity. The human body encompassed five points, the head and extremities; and the hand itself had five fingers. The graphic chain of form had a dynamic impact on human's attempt to understand their role in the universe.

Life force entered through the fingertips and took up residence in the hand in the various mounts. If an abundance of this force gathered in any one spot, then that spot would swell up with power and become elevated, or a mount. As centers of energy, the mounts came to represent our talents and personal potential. Each mount came to represent a specific force.

As far as the division of the forces goes, it is hard to say which came first in palmistry: the recognition of the zones of the hand and a consequent pattern of naming the energies or a pre-existing division of energy leading to the formation of the zones and quadrants. The ancient, instinctive division of existence into heaven, earth, and hell, or into divine, human, and baser categories, applied to the hand, just as it applied to everything humanity tried to capture and understand.

The only thing we know for certain is that palmistry had to have been a highly evolved study, possibly an exact science related to the human body and aspirations, because the meanings ascribed to the mounts demonstrate an explicit understanding of human nature and energy. Just how early in history humanity arrived at this is not known.

The mounts and energies are divided among the active and passive, conscious and unconscious zones (see Diagrams B and C, p. 107). They also share in the threefold division of heaven, earth, and hell.

Jupiter, Saturn, Apollo, and Mercury are mounts of social energy in the active zone of the hand (Diagram A, p. 107), while Venus, Luna, Neptune, and Pluto belong to the lower, instinctive energy zone in the passive section of the hand (Diagram B). The fingers are the flowering of the energy of the mounts and represent the mental zone. The two Mars mounts are on the active-passive dividing line; one falls in the conscious, the other in the unconscious zone. Saturn, the Plain of Mars, and Neptune embrace both the conscious and the unconscious zones (Diagram C).

Each mount (Diagram D, p. 107) contains a certain kind of energy and talent. For the mount to be defined as a good mount, the area should be firm to the touch and be elevated. A flat area where the mount should be means that the energy that should be there is deficient. Talents and potential that accompany that mount are absent. If a mount is very, very high, the energy is overdeveloped and can point to excesses. If a mount is high, its meaning should not be viewed entirely negatively, for the excess energy can be channeled and directed positively. Neither should a flat mount be interpreted as a dead end, because other talents and interests can be developed.

THE JUPITER MOUNT

Jupiter is the name of the chief of the Roman gods. He stood for supreme authority and was a guiding light whose influence extended to these roles: statesman, diplomat, teacher, and protector of children and animals. He was a hearty character with a love of life that is reflected in our English word, "jovial."

A good Mount of Jupiter. All of these qualities are reflected in a good Mount of Jupiter. This mount indicates a potential for leadership and forceful communication of knowledge, a love of authority, the ability to teach, and a love of animals.

The Jupiter person is optimistic and philosophical. A good mount means splendid powers of self-projection. Whichever talent or interest this person focuses on is developed with flair and self-assurance.

A flat Mount of Jupiter, especially if it is combined with a short index finger, involves problems stemming from lack of enthusiasm and a possible inferiority complex. The self-assurance associated with Jupiter is not there, nor is the faith necessary for sticking to projects when the going gets rough.

As a palmist you can counsel clients with a flat Mount of Jupiter to help them find something that will arouse and command their interest. This starting point can provide motivation to help sweep these people from their lethargy. Sometimes the support of another person who acts as a sympathetic listener or partner will be enough to prod these people into action.

An overdeveloped mount. If the mount is overdeveloped, you will need to point out to these people the wisdom of a low-key approach. A soft-sell of all their talents and a toning down of their enthusiasm at times will make them able to approach others with success.

THE MOUNT OF SATURN

The Mount of Saturn lies next to Jupiter on one side, and extends to a point midway between the middle and ring fingers on the other side. It extends down to the heart line in depth.

This mount also shares the unique qualities of the Saturn finger, which is the dividing line between the zones representing the conscious and unconscious minds. This position makes the mount a particularly sensitive one. Perhaps for this reason it has had a number of far-reaching or esoteric meanings attributed to it. It is best to remember only that it is a sensitive point, encompassing a balance of both the conscious and unconscious worlds. If there is a war between these worlds in an individual psyche, it will be reflected in this mount. The mount will be highly developed, marking the presence and function of unusual energies, but it doesn't follow from this that a large Saturn mount has to mean a melancholy or unbalanced individual.

A reason such meanings have been given to this mount is the nature of Saturn itself. Saturn is Father Time, Cronos, and a teacher of hard and inevitable lessons. The work of Saturn progresses slowly but surely. These qualities can be interpreted positively, for there is a certain satisfaction in contemplating fulfillment and work that is completed.

Highly developed, the Mount of Saturn indicates a very sensitive personality. What may seem like a gloomy perspective to others may only be, in reality, a different way of looking at things. A saturnine personality is frequently out of step with its peers, and small wonder, for he will be concerned more than the average with balance and adjustment. For people who rarely give these things a thought, this turn of mind will seem strange. A saturnine personality in many cases is engaged in a search, a search for wisdom and knowledge. This could lead to occult views, and a talent for the occult is associated with the Saturn mount, if it is developed at all. Such a talent is a possibility but not guaranteed with this mount, for there is a larger significance. If Saturn is associated with searching, it is also associated with a process, a process of becoming and evolving.

Highly developed Saturn mounts are found on people who deeply appreciate music. This could stem from the deeper concern for harmony. Very observant people also have well-developed Mounts of Saturn.

Because of the unusual preoccupations the saturnine personality is bound to have, there is the possibility of a perception of the tragic sense of life. It can't be denied that the evolutionary process associated with Saturn sometimes leads to this perception, but along the way many unusual insights are gained, and the saturnine personality may have something to offer that will elevate others' awareness. Saturn types cannot be dismissed as messengers of gloom and doom.

A flat Mount of Saturn means a quieter state of affairs for the conscious and unconscious mind. Achieving balance between the two is not such a crucial issue or struggle. At times values are accepted or chosen haphazardly. A flat Saturn mount doesn't by itself signify apathy, but perhaps a restful state of mind.

It wouldn't hurt for those with flat Saturn mounts to prepare themselves for another day in which they may wake up to deeper realities and be surprised by what they see. Values will no longer be chosen haphazardly.

A long Saturn finger and a well-developed mount will indicate too much of a good thing and will be associated with a feeling of estrangement from others, rather than with an unusual or viable philosophy of life.

The opposite of this condition, a flat Saturn mount and short middle finger, means little ability to plan for the future. People with this type of mount and finger can't imagine having to worry about the future. The positive feature is that any tendency to worry will be blissfully absent.

THE APOLLO MOUNT

The traits associated with the Apollo mount represent quite a radical departure from those indicated by the Saturn mount. The Apollo mount indicates powers of creativity and fulfillment. There is genuine joy, a joy that is the result of productivity. The concern for today that is felt by the Apollo type is matched by an equal concern for the future. Questions or feelings about immortality are often a part of the Apollo personality. Creation for these people is a way to perpetuate themselves and to share their knowledge. Sharing, warmth, laughter, caring for and loving others are traits of the Apollo person. Apollo is the sun god in mythology, who radiates all these qualities and is the essence of the creator.

There is often a feeling that Apollo people are blessed with divine guidance, a sense that their creations reflect the divine itself. There is a tremendous power in this mount, and a type of power that is not easily explained, since it stems from the unconscious. Perhaps this is why Apollo has traditionally been called the lucky mount, but to call it lucky is to miss the point. Things don't just happen, for it is the individual power and vitality that does the work.

We have to remember that this mount is the first of the mounts in the active area of the hand to fall completely inside the unconscious zone. It is the active expression of the powers of the unconscious. Apollo is bounded by Saturn on one side and by Mercury on the other. It extends in depth to the heart line.

A well-developed Mount of Apollo signals creativity, a spark of life that is unusual, a flair and presence that make themselves felt. At times this flair expresses itself in an artistic nature. This is likely since a good Apollo mount belongs to a person who has an above-average appreciation for form, color, texture, and linear harmony.

With **a flat Mount of Apollo**, a person is not so inclined to be creative. A well-developed mount, since it is associated with Apollo, often depicted as wreathed in laurels and playing a lyre, indicates a need to be noticed and appreciated. In the case of a flat mount, the person is satisfied to stay out of the limelight.

A very flat Apollo mount combined with a short ring finger means that the person is very retiring. Any effort you can make as a palmist to awaken this person to the positive aspects of creating something new or enjoying the arts will bring about rewarding experiences the person had never dreamed of before. A flat mount does not put a final lid on the ability to be creative. It means that something or someone must awaken this person to the desire to create or to new forms of beauty.

THE MERCURY MOUNT

Mercury is known as Hermes, the winged messenger, and all the qualities of the Mercury mount stem from this role and its implied characteristics: swiftness, a sense of urgent communication, dealings with others that extend to trade and commerce, speaking ability, eloquence, and shrewdness.

With a messenger there is transmission of knowledge and perhaps secrets. The "secret sciences" of the occult and healing are very much a part of this mount. Also associated with this mount are aptitude for medicine and science and for the understanding of nature's laws.

No matter what area of mercurian interests the client chooses, a well-developed Mercury mount means that a quick mind and swiftness of comprehension are applied to the task. Mercurian thoughts are as agile as the feet of Hermes, the messenger.

Good Mercury mounts. People who have strong Mercury mounts make good teachers, reporters, journalists, photographers, and travelers. Many mercurians are mediums, either because they are practiced in the occult, or simply because of a natural ability to be the means through which some form of knowledge and learning is transmitted.

The type of career suited to your client with a strong Mercury mount can be seen through the sections of the fingers. If the top sections are long, there is an inclination to teach and work with ideas. With the second sections long, there will be an aptitude and interest in science and medicine. When the bottom sections are longest, business ability is indicated.

A very large Mercury mount, one that overshadows the other mounts, is in itself a sign of ambition. To see what lines the ambition will take, check the finger sections again.

A flat Mercury mount has no particular negative connotation. It means that this person will not be naturally interested in medicine or business, although he or she could enter these fields if other signs in the hand—such as the length of the fingers—indicate an inclination to be thorough and painstaking, and if he or she gets proper training. Although a well-developed mount always shows a lively person, the person with a flat mount is not dull. The reverse does not hold here.

Negative traits and well-developed Mercury mounts. Whenever you do find a well-developed Mount of Mercury, you know that this person operates on hunches very often, if not exclusively. Long fingers would show an ability to hold this tendency in check, while short fingers would indicate an exaggeration of the tendency.

Because Mercurians can be very shrewd, and because the Mercury mount often signals an interest in business, some of the negative implications of these two areas have been reinforced and have grown out of proportion. Specifically, a strong Mount of Mercury does not mean that a person is an unqualified cheat, thief, or deceiver of others who are not so quick. As with all abilities, Mercury abilities can be misused, but the tendency to see cheaters or clever crooks in those with prominent Mercury mounts or long Mercury fingers calls for caution. If a Mercurian has a tendency to be deceptive, that tendency will be supported in other parts of the hand. The thumb may be weak, the coloring of the hand deficient, or the head line disturbed. These would be some supporting clues.

If you find these signs you might want to find out why the person feels a need to be shrewd or evasive. Talking to the person may bring some interesting reasons to light.

Very long Mercury fingers and a strong mount mean above-average communication skills. How they are used depends on the person, but everyone could learn from these people. At a minimum, everyone could increase verbal skills by listening to and understanding the Mercury type.

THE DIFFERENCE BETWEEN MOUNTS IN THE ACTIVE AND PASSIVE ZONES

All four of the mounts just studied—Jupiter, Saturn, Apollo, and Mercury—are in the active zone of the hand. That is why they are so useful for determining interests, talents, and potential, for these mounts' qualities will be expressed if the mounts are developed. This area of the hand shows very clearly what a person is prepared to communicate and act out on an everyday level.

When we come to the mounts in the lower or instinctive zone, we are entering the passive section of the hand, and the talents these mounts show are not always expressed on an everyday basis. Expression is a more subtle process. Some or all of the talents contained in the lower mounts will be used according to individual potential seen in other areas of the hand. For instance, the harmony seen in a good Mount of Venus will have many avenues of expression.

THE MOUNT OF VENUS

Because the Mount of Venus forms the root of the thumb and a substantial section of the hand itself, it is interpreted as the source of vitality and power. The Mount of Venus is the prime indicator of your client's energy. What type of vitality does he or she have at their command: physical, mental, or emotional?

A flat Mount of Venus means that the person's energy is channeled along mental lines. A well-developed mount means abundant physical energy, and a very high mount shows much emotional energy.

In a very general and simple view, the mount shows *how much* energy a person has. It follows logically that as the mount increases in size, physical energy is greater, and if there is a great deal of physical energy, the person has enough left over to pour into their emotions. A pink coloring on the mount will increase emotional energy.

The Mount of Venus is bounded by the life line, and in the chapter on this line, the width of the path of this line in the hand will be seen as an indicator of vitality.

The well-developed mount. The more highly developed the mount is, the greater energy a person has to work with. In the case of a well-developed mount, the energy carries the person along, making him or her joyous, warm, and fun-loving. People with a good Venus mount are gifted with physical grace, and often are dancers and athletes. There is a love of music associated with this mount.

People with a wide or high Mount of Venus are very aware of the rhythm of life, of the harmony and instinctive patterns in the flow of life. This awareness can be expressed artistically, or it may show up as a preoccupation with harmonious relationships between the self and others, or between the self and the environment. The gracefulness associated with Venus may be expressed mentally, especially if the mount is developed moderately.

The flat mount. When your client has a very flat-looking Mount of Venus, or a soft mount, the potential for liveliness and a sense of fun has to be developed. This can be done by increasing physical vitality. This person above all needs to get more physical exercise. As he or she exercises, the mount will become firmer or higher. In the same way, a new outlook and an increased interest in life will cause changes in the mount. The import of a flat mount is a lower level of energy and the main issue is what can be done to increase this level.

THE MOUNT OF LUNA

The Mount of Luna is a very interesting one. It falls in the unconscious and passive zone of the hand. This is very appropriate, for the function of Luna is mainly its role as a storehouse. What is stored is memory of all types: childhood, ancestral, and racial memories.

This mount is traditionally associated with writing ability, dreamy creativity, and water. Memory of all types makes it possible to write, to dream, and to create. The watery element of Luna is quite apropos, for this mount embraces memories that date from the womb and before, extending back to the primordial state of humankind.

The well-developed mount. If this mount is highly padded in the palm of the hand itself, writing and creative ability are indicated.

The outward-curving mount. At times, the mount is curved outward on the edge of the hand (Diagram E, p. 108). This shows a love of water that will draw the person to live by lakes, rivers, streams, or the ocean. Sometimes an outward-curving mount is found on the hands of navigators.

The bulging outward curve. The curve that refers to a love of water is always gently and evenly rounded. If the curve on the outside of the hand has a noticeable bulge in one spot and is rather flat by comparison for the rest of the mount, then something else altogether is indicated.

The three types of memory and their importance for the person are seen in this type of bulge at the outer edge of the hand. For all practical purposes, divide Luna into three sections (Diagram F, p. 108) and label them 1, 2, and 3.

A bulge in section 1. The first section, which is closest to the active section of the hand, contains childhood memories, memories that can be drawn up to the surface pretty much at will. There is more conscious control over these memories, for they are what have been experienced firsthand by the person.

A bulge in section 2. Section 2, if it bulges outward, means that ancestral memories influence the person. Stories heard about the ancestors will have an impact. Even more, with this bulge, there is quite often a love and reverence for ancestors that is instinctive. People with this bulge are likely to research family history and to possess a talent for genealogical studies.

The important thing with this curve is that love of ancestors influences the person, perhaps unconsciously. If a deliberate acquaintance with ancestors hasn't been sought yet, any knowledge of them will help these persons understand why they act as they do or prefer the things they do in many cases.

A bulge in section 3. Section 3 refers to the most remote memory of all. Racial memories always have a special appeal for this person. This section means a talent for ancient history, archeology, or philosophy. There is a preoccupation with the origin of humankind and the universe. If your client has a bulge at this section of their hand, they will probably already have given some thought to primeval states, having pictured the planet inhabited by cavemen, prehistoric animals, and strange vegetation. A concern for the link between humans and animals, or for the creation of being, marks the thought of this person.

If this third section is well developed, there is often a crease just above the padding (Diagram G, p. 108). This crease traditionally has stood for a love of voyages, mental or physical. This fits in well with the racial memories that might inspire such traveling.

The developed mount. Any development of the Mount of Luna means an active unconscious life. The unconscious voice wants to be heard, and its speech does not assume ordinary verbal patterns. Most often the unconscious speaks in symbols, and a developed Mount of Luna shows an interest in symbols, a talent for poetry, and a love of variety and change. It is a rich sign that can point to a restless person, for having heard the voice of the unconscious, this person may not be content with everyday or mundane realities.

For this reason, a high Mount of Luna has been interpreted as signifying a restless nature or a desire for escape. Both of these qualities can be productive. The focus of Luna is creativity. Whatever you can say that will encourage and discipline the Luna type to use his or her creative potential can bring positive experiences.

THE MARS MOUNTS

Discipline, motivation, and self-control are qualities of the Mars mounts. Study these to find out what needs to be developed for facilitating the creativity of Luna.

The two Mars mounts are situated very close to the dividing line between the active and passive areas of the hand (Diagram H, p. 109). One of the mounts falls in the conscious zone and the other in the unconscious zone. Because of this difference in placement, the same basic meaning of courage and drive is applied differently in interpreting each mount.

Upper Mars belongs on the unconscious side of the hand and so it shows a type of bravery that is instinctive and a reaction to events. Lower Mars, situated on the active side of the hand, right beside the thumb, speaks of initiative. Both mounts show how much courage a person has and how he or she will use it.

A very well-developed Mount of Mars at the thumb area shows courage in beginning new projects and indicates ambition. Successful salespeople and business people nearly always have a developed Mars mount here.

A flat mount. If the area is flat (Diagram I, p. 109), then the person hasn't got enough ambition and will need something to stimulate the drive to succeed. A flat area means that the person is not motivated. Initiative will have to be developed.

Developed upper Mars. If upper Mars, on the outer edge of the hand, is developed (Diagram I), the client is revealed to be consistent and enduring in whatever has been undertaken. Such development also means that the person does not go to pieces in a crisis. A certain kind of bravery keeps him or her from being dismayed or upset when things don't go well. He or she simply doesn't scare easily.

Flat upper Mars. If this part of the hand is flat, showing no development at all, then the person has given in to the fearful side of his nature. When he or she is faced with something new, there is an initial reaction of fear or the feeling that they can't cope.

When you find that your client has a flat Mount of Mars here, talk over with her or him the necessity of a calmer attitude. They will feel better if they can learn to wait before reacting and if they can learn to persevere. Steady reactions and an unruffled outlook will really benefit them.

Contrasting mounts. If the lower Mount of Mars by the thumb is high, in contrast to the other mount, the person will start many new projects without finishing them. There is ambition to initiate but nothing with which to follow through. This sign calls for cultivation of a more reliable nature. Just finishing one real project or job can help this person realize the satisfaction of finishing a job, and perhaps make it easier to complete the next.

If upper Mars is developed and the thumb-area Mars flat, clients may be too stolid or set in a pattern that doesn't inspire action. The positive side is their calm and enduring nature, but the bonus is to get them moving on something new!

Equally developed mounts. Both Mars mounts should have nearly equal development so that the person's energies, however small or great, are evenly distributed.

These mounts provide a channel for the distribution of energy flowing from the passive to the active sections and back. The regulation of the upward flow of the instinctual energies, their expression according to the mounts under the fingers, and the return of fulfilled energy is indicated to some extent by these Mars mounts. They are checkpoints and you can think of them this way, for they occupy a position on the borderline.

You can think of these Mars mounts as filling stations, complete with a sign that says "last gas station for one hundred and fifty miles." The energy in these mounts has to be enough to last for the trip to and from the active mounts under the fingers.

The Plain of Mars. The very middle of the palm is called the Plain of Mars. Many of the traits seen in the other two Mars mounts used to be read here. The center of the hand is still important, for it is an area where all the energies from the various mounts come together. More research has to be done on this area. When you are reading it, interpret it according to its thick or thin appearance (chapter ten, pages 65–66).

THE MOUNT OF NEPTUNE

The Neptune mount lies at the bottom of the hand between Venus and Luna (Diagram B). In this position it encompasses the dividing line between the conscious and unconscious zones, while at the same time it is in the passive section. This is an appropriate location, for the action of Neptune's qualities is never direct or straightforward. The blend of the conscious and unconscious life, which receives instinctive rather than active expression, fits Neptune very well.

When the Mount of Neptune is developed, its bulge at the bottom center of the hand creates a prominent ridge across the entire base of the palm by linking the Mounts of Venus and Luna. Whenever present, this ridge is readily detected by the eye.

Neptune is the planet synonymous with camouflage or deception, the mysterious or enchanting. There is a hypnotic quality to its characteristics.

The developed mount. People with a developed Mount of Neptune have the ability to captivate an audience. This is helpful for actors, but this mount is also found on people who can lecture to large groups of people and hold their attention, whether the subject is entertaining or not.

When you find this mount on a client, try asking about his or her experience with speaking to groups of people. If they have tried it, more than likely they have been comfortable with it. Perhaps they haven't had an occasion to stand up in front of a group of people and don't know that it can be done, but if the mount is there, the ability is there, and can be used anytime.

The flat mount. When the Neptune mount is flat or undeveloped, this doesn't mean that the person can't speak to groups. Other qualities, such as those indicated by a good Jupiter mount (self-projection) or a good Mercury mount (liveliness and wit), can do the job.

THE MOUNT OF PLUTO

Recently, the third section of Luna has been given the name of Pluto. So far, not much practical interpretation has been given to this mount. The mount can signify an interest and ability in the occult. This is a possible interpretation; a talent for the occult is more likely to be present if the mount is developed than if it isn't. Pluto as a planet is famous for symbolizing the power of regeneration. This meaning, combined with the strong sense of racial memory in this section of the hand, could point to a person who is able to teach the world something of ancient truths or ancient knowledge.

In a sense, the Mount of Pluto is a deeper continuation of the powers of creativity found in Luna. Time will provide other meanings for this mount.

OVERALL MOUNT DEVELOPMENT

Each hand will have a certain mount development. Some of the mounts will be flat, others padded. When you are reading hands, notice which zone of the hand has developed mounts, and you will know immediately how your client operates and on what level. This knowledge is invaluable for a good analysis. It helps in understanding the other person, too, and can be useful in your personal life as well.

It takes time to be able to put the meanings of the mounts together into clear focus, but once you are able to recognize the type of energy they represent, and which of them is the strongest, you will have a key to personality and individual potential.

THE MOUNTS

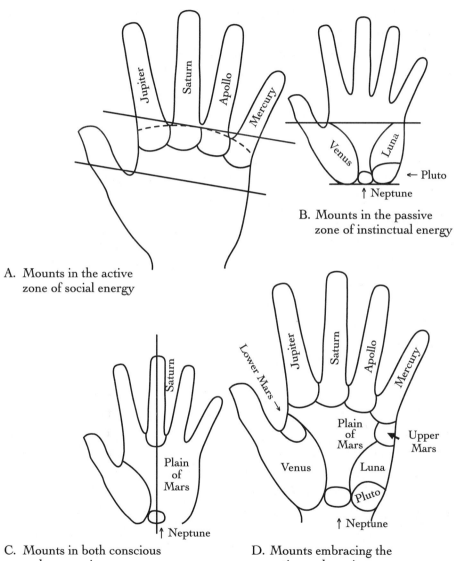

A. Mounts in the active
   zone of social energy

B. Mounts in the passive
   zone of instinctual energy

C. Mounts in both conscious
   and unconscious zones

D. Mounts embracing the
   active and passive zones

THE MOUNTS

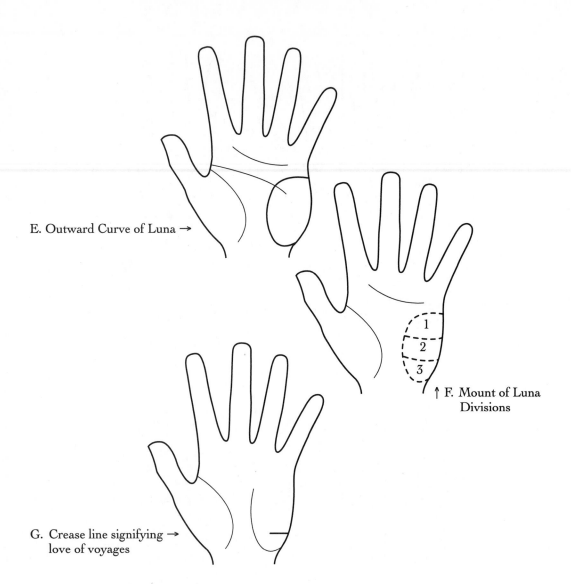

E. Outward Curve of Luna →

↑ F. Mount of Luna
Divisions

G. Crease line signifying →
love of voyages

THE MOUNTS

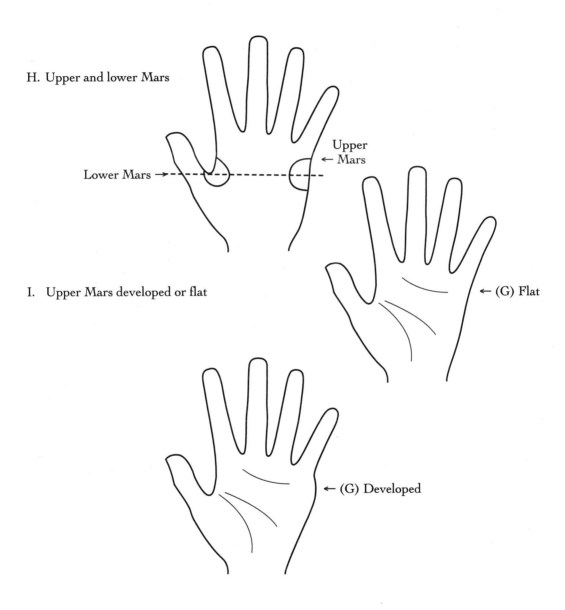

H. Upper and lower Mars

Lower Mars →

Upper
← Mars

I. Upper Mars developed or flat

← (G) Flat

← (G) Developed

14

Marking the Mounts and Lines

Special markings are found on both the mounts and the lines. These marks have certain forms, some of which apply to both mounts and lines, while others belong just to mounts or just to lines. These markings increase the significance and add to the interpretation of lines and mounts. Mounts especially take on added meaning if marks appear on them, for they are smooth areas that in most cases do not require the presence of tiny lines.

MARKINGS ON THE MOUNTS

There are at least ten types of marks that can be found on the mounts (Diagram A, p. 116). Many times there will be only a single mark or line, but any line on a mount must be read for the direction it takes.

Vertical lines. A vertical line is a positive sign, while a horizontal line (when it is not a major line) indicates a hindrance of the energy associated with the mounts. Visualize it as a block to the flow of the mount's energy.

Vertical lines on the mounts of **Jupiter, Saturn, and Apollo** increase the positive interpretations of the mounts. **On Mercury**, three vertical lines (Diagram B, p. 116) mean special healing ability. **Venus**: a series of vertical lines on Venus at the bottom of the mount means that the person has achieved a sense of balance, grace, or art. They indicate an increase in the flow of energy associated with the mount.

Slanting lines. Vertical lines on Luna are rare. However, a series of slanted lines on Luna (/ / /) shows the influence of people who act as advisors to this person. With these slanting lines there is a desire to cooperate and to please others.

Jupiter. Slanting lines aren't found on Venus but they often occur on **Jupiter** (Diagram C, p. 116). Slanting from Jupiter to Saturn, they mean either that the person has been in a career situation where rank was important or that he or she is close to someone who has been in that situation.

Horizontal lines. Short horizontal lines on **Venus** indicate an obstacle to the free flow of energy. A longer horizontal line that starts inside the life line on Venus and continues out into the palm (Diagram D, p. 117) shows a private affair or conflict brought out into the open. If the line extends from Venus to Mercury (Diagram E, p. 117), it is a sure sign of separation from a loved one or a marriage partner.

Luna. Horizontal lines on Luna traditionally refer to health problems involving the intestines, bladder, or kidneys. If the lines are found only on the outer edge of Luna, and not on the palm itself, they mean restlessness (Diagram F, p. 117). The person feels that he or she is not using their abilities wisely or constructively. A very long horizontal line near the bottom third of Luna, on the palm itself, is an allergy line (Diagram G, p. 117). It shows an intolerance to certain anesthetics, drugs, or alcohol.

Grilles, cross-hatched lines, can occur on any mount and they intensify the meaning of the mount. They are a sign of hyperactivity or excessive needs. Picture the confusion in the lines running in a patch at cross purposes. The vertical or positive lines meet and cross horizontal or obstacle lines. The mixing of these little channels that signify either a reinforcement or a hindrance of the flow of energy heightens the activity and characteristics of the mount they mark. Needs or tendencies in the mounts become intensified: the need for love, in the case of **Venus;** the need to have authority, in the case of **Jupiter;** on **Saturn,** a tendency to brood; on **Apollo,** a tendency to show off; and on **Mercury,** shrewdness or glibness. A grille on **Luna** can mean a health problem in the stomach or lower intestines. A grille on **upper Mars** means that certain types of arthritis seem to run in the family. A grille on **lower Mars** indicates a rather bellicose spirit and a tendency to be quarrelsome.

Crosses on the mounts have more specific or limited readings. Traditional meanings are:

- **On Venus:** a union for love but seldom happy.
- **On Saturn:** tragedy.
- **On Apollo:** frustration.
- **On Mercury:** writing ability.
- **On Jupiter:** a happy marriage.
- **On Luna:** overactive imagination.

Squares on the mounts are a positive sign. They mean a feeling of security in whatever the mount represents. When a square is found on **Jupiter,** individuals are so secure in their knowledge that they are able to share it easily. Hence it is called the "teacher's square." Such a square is seen not only on teachers' hands, but on anyone whose position requires them to explain or demonstrate something. A foreman will often have this sign, as well as a home fashion demonstrator, or those who lecture to the public for humanitarian causes.

Triangles have specific meanings. On **Saturn,** a triangle means a gift for the occult or an aptitude for serious studies. On **Jupiter,** it is a sign of unusual diplomacy and tact. On **Apollo,** it means a craftsman or genius; on **Mercury,** a love of ad-libs, and on **Luna,** a gift of prophecy and intuition. On **Mars,** a triangle has been said to mean military genius. Triangles, whether on the mounts as a separate sign or formed by patterns in the main lines, indicate unusual skill and genius. Think of them as signifying talent. With this in mind, an additional meaning for a triangle on Mars might be extraordinary endurance or bravery in a number of situations, including the traditional military significance given to it.

Both circles and stars are unusual signs on the mounts. **Circles** are truly seldom seen—so seldom, in fact, that meanings for them are not really verified. Traditionally, a circle on Apollo means fame.

Stars actually resemble asterisks. To be a true star, the configuration should have six or more equally strong lines: $\asterisk$, and not be sketchily formed, so that the eye has to fill in the details.

These stars are at times overrated. Traditional meanings make them omens of great fortune or great tragedy. Research is needed in this area, too, to complete a sensible definition of stars. Can they really augur wonderful surprises or point to the depths of despair? If so, why are they found on people who lead very ordinary lives, who perhaps don't even dream of changing those lives? It would seem that these little asterisks increase the energy signified by the mount, but to limit their interpretation to a single meaning per mount seems foolhardy. Two of these stars have traditionally positive meanings, and they could form the basis for more research: on Jupiter, a star indicates a happy or wealthy marriage; on Apollo, sudden fame.

MARKINGS ON THE LINES

There are six frequently found markings on the lines (Diagram H, p. 118). Of these, the bar is the most common, perhaps followed by the dot and square. Crosses sometimes occur, while the star and triangle are quite rare.

The bar marks a hindrance in the function of the line. It means an obstacle, but an obstacle that is not felt over a long period of time. **Crosses,** which signify specific problems, point to problems of longer duration. Meanings for crosses on or alongside the lines will be given in the chapters on lines. **Dots** reveal interruptions in the energy flow of the line and can relate to specific but minor health problems, as also delineated in the following chapters. **Stars and triangles** mean "agitation" and "ingenuity," respectively. **Squares** signify protection.

The lines themselves have special formations that define their appearance. Although lines should be clearly sketched on the hand, and free of the following forms, they rarely are picture-perfect. Actually, the deviation from the ideal appearance is what gives the lines their various meanings. The special formations characterizing the lines include depth, chains, islands, tassels, breaks, and branches. Diagram I illustrates four of these formations.

Deep lines. Lines are channels for the forces—mental, physical, and emotional—that make up the individual. The lines should be clear and fairly deeply etched in the hand. Deep lines are a sign of vitality and endurance. A deep **head line** means the ability to concentrate, a deep **heart line** shows retention of emotional experiences, and a deep **life line** signals good physical vitality. All of these will be explored more at length in later chapters.

Lighter lines are sometimes so pale that the palmist will have to stretch the hand to see what path they take in the hand. This is always a sign of a weaker, but not necessarily sickly, physical constitution, and of a tendency to worry. It also means that the person is sensitive and needs more sleep than the average to recover from the impact of daily, waking life.

The variations in the lines' appearance can be classed according to meaning. Chains, islands, breaks, and tassels (Diagram I, p. 118) mean difficulties. They signify a power break-down, or in lesser cases a need for adjustment. Forces represented in the lines will have to accommodate themselves to the form of the line.

Chains signify confusion. There is a disturbance of the energies represented by the lines.

Islands. With an island, the power symbolically splits in two, takes two directions, and then returns to a single source. This diversion means both a weakening of the line and a feeling of confinement in the realm the line represents. In the case of the life line, an island shows a period of poor health and either actual confinement or a feeling of confinement because of health. Islands on the heart line or head line can point to poor physical health, but they also can mean emotional or mental upsets.

A **tassel** at the end of the line means a complete breakdown or scattering of the line's power. There is a weakness in the line. A tassel is a rare occurrence.

Many times tassels can be confused with rising or descending lines (Diagram J, p. 118). The way to tell them apart lies in the fact that a tassel occurs only at the end of the line. It is similar in appearance to a bunch of lines squeezed together, much like straws on a broomstick.

Forked lines. If the line should have a fork on it (Diagram K, p. 118), its meaning and power are increased in all cases but the life line. On the life line, a fork is said to diminish the power.

Forks can be either two-pronged or triple-pronged. The triple prong is unusual and greatly increases the good meaning of the head and heart lines.

Branching lines. A whole series of tiny lines can branch off the main lines. Rising branch lines (Diagram L, p. 118) are positive signs; descending branch lines, which head for the bottom of the hand (Diagram L), point to a decrease in the power of the line and an element of disappointment or energy misspent.

Breaks also occur on lines. Specific meanings for breaks and all the other markings are given in the chapters dealing with the major lines.

MARKINGS ON MOUNTS

A. Markings on the mounts

|| Vertical lines   ✕   Cross

=   Horizontal lines   ⊞ ☐   Squares

///   Slanting lines   △ △   Triangles

—   Single bar line   ◌ ○   Circles

▦   Grille   ✳   Star

B. Healing lines on Mercury →

C. Slanting lines from
    Jupiter to Saturn →

MARKINGS ON MOUNTS

D. Line inside Venus
continues into palm ↓

E. Line inside Venus continues to Mercury mount →

F. Lines of
restlessness on
outer edge of hand →

G. Allergy line ↑

H. Markings on lines

I. Variations in lines' appearance

J. Rising and descending lines and tassels

Rising lines   Descending lines   Tassels

K. Forked Lines   Forked line — dual prong

Forked line — triple prong

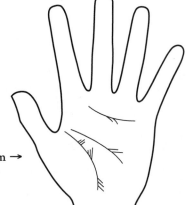

L. Small lines rising or descending from →
main lines

15

The Life Line

With the major lines, we are looking at a genetic record. These lines were formed in the first sixteen weeks of life and reflect all that is inherited from our ancestors—temperament, type of intelligence, and physical vitality.

The major lines are the heart, head, and life lines (Diagram A, p. 128), and these lines are normally the deepest lines in the hand. They travel through every zone of the hand and form a complete expression of an individual's energy and potential.

WHAT THE LIFE LINE SHOWS

Basic vitality. The most important line, the life line, indicates basic vitality, while the other two tell how this energy is channeled. By comparing the depth of all three major lines, the type of energy that predominates can be seen: mental, physical, or emotional.

The life line is not the death line. More misconceptions surround the life line than any other line. The poor line is notorious, and often the first question a person asks a palm reader is "How long will I live?"

That anyone would ask such a question of another person is rather frightening. Worse still is the fact that many people attempt to answer it.

There may be real occasions of need when this question arises, or perhaps the question reflects nothing but idle curiosity. No matter what the motivation is, under no circumstances should anyone attempt a direct answer. Answers to this question have ruined many nights of sleep and done incalculable harm.

If there is any doubt in your mind, as a palmist, why you should not predict dates of death or assign a length of life to anyone, try this test. Imagine for a moment that you have, through some marvelous means, the date of your own death. No matter what your reaction to this information is, it colors your awareness and the living out of your remaining days. If you had the fact of your own death as a specific, unalterable date, it would be like any other engagement. It is on your calendar, and you have to plan around it.

Now imagine that you are the poor, innocent person who has been led to believe that another person has the power to look into the future and pick out your death date, single it out from all the billions of predestined death dates existing from time immemorial till the end of time. It seems inconceivable that anyone could believe that another person has the ability to see such a thing.

Predicting the date of death is a weak point in palmistry precisely because, in the past, accommodating readers and their worried clients were not strong enough to stand up and say, "This is impossible!" The knowledge of the future was too tempting. It helped to relieve them of responsibility for their actions and allowed them to blame their difficulties on an unchangeable fate.

With questions about the length of life, all sense of proportion is lost. The question is put to another human being, who is then asked to play God. Perhaps today our awareness that "you get what you pay for" will save us from asking such a question. In everyday life the purchase of a cheap product is no bargain. Trading a human guess for the unknowable produces a poor warranty. The clause of suspense and doubt never runs out.

Health. Whenever there is a need to know about health and the probable life span it entails, the palmist can focus on the health and vitality inherited from ancestors. This can be seen in the life line. At all times, prevention and medical attention can help any hereditary weaknesses. The hand, if it is interpreted properly, can be of assistance in diagnosing unhealthy tendencies and in proposing steps to offset these tendencies.

Psychological traits and changes in lifestyle. There are other meanings to the life line. In addition to physical vitality, certain psychological traits can be seen, and because the life line reflects a person's heredity, any breaks or changes in the course of the line can indicate a break with tradition and the lifestyles known by the family. A break in the life line doesn't always refer to health matters.

Since the information from the life line covers diverse areas, it is helpful to consider a condensation of what this line can tell:

- Approximate timing for events and experiences.
- Past accidents or sickness.
- Future health potential.
- Certain personality traits: introversion, extroversion, ambivalence, ambition, and restlessness.
- Change of homes or geographical location.
- Changes in lifestyle.

In summary, the life line indicates physical vitality and the probable course a life will take.

GENERAL CHARACTERISTICS OF THE LIFE LINE

The life line begins at the edge of the hand, by the thumb, at a point midway between the thumb and the Mount of Jupiter (Diagram B, p. 128). It swings around the thumb and normally reaches to the end of the hand.

The wide arc. The arc made by the line as it travels down the hand may be very wide, cutting halfway into the hand, or very narrow, appearing to hug the thumb.

When the life line swings out in a naturally wide arc into the hand (Diagram C, p. 128), extroversion is indicated. The person with such a life line enjoys people and takes what comes along with good humor or in stride, having enough energy to cope with whatever befalls him or her.

The narrow arc. If the line is narrow (Diagram C, dotted extension), the scope of vitality is limited, and also consequently is the energy available for social relationships. The narrow line nearly always corresponds with an introverted personality. Part of the reason for this is that these people have less energy to work with and, as a consequence, things don't come easily to them. They can't keep up with as many activities as a wider course to the life line indicates.

A short life line, which ends before it reaches the bottom of the hand (Diagram D, p. 128), means that the physical vitality is limited, that perhaps the client's ancestors died at an earlier age than the norm, but it in no way implies a person's own length of life. Any deficiency in physical vitality can be compensated for by other good signs in the hand, as well as by practical measures in life. If the line is short on the dominant hand, or on both hands, the person is likely, at one point in life, to function more on nerves than on true physical strength.

A long life line (Diagram D, dotted extension) indicates good physical vitality if there aren't other marks indicating weakness, but this inherited tendency for a long life or good physical strength can be changed by poor living habits, careless attitudes, or by accidents that occur after the line is formed. A life line's potential for good health can be short-circuited by any number of circumstances. This line is a sign of a good inheritance genetically, but it isn't an unconditional guarantee.

The broken arc: narrow-wide. A life line that begins in a narrow arc (Diagram E, p. 129) and ends after a short path, only to be followed by another line with a wider arc, shows that this lifestyle will not be the same as a parents' or family's. Either these individuals will progress far beyond their initial circumstances in life and know an entirely different type of world, or they will travel to another geographical location.

In the case of people who have forged different lifestyles or moved far away from home and whose life lines do not have this change in course, the lack of a course change will mean an emotional attachment to the past, in spite of the changes made.

A line that breaks and changes course means a clean break with the past.

The broken arc: wide-narrow. Very rarely you will find a life line that starts with a wide arc, stops, and continues in a narrower arc (Diagram F, p. 129). This also indicates a change in lifestyle, but it shows a reverse of a wide arc: restrictions in outlook and lifestyle.

The broken arc: segmented. Sometimes a life line will be found to have several sections, perhaps three or more, with breaks in between (Diagram G, p. 129). The course the new and succeeding lines follow is important. Does the arc remain consistent, or does it become broader or narrower? As with Diagram E, any tendency for the arc to become wider means a chance for change in lifestyle. If there are many sections to the life line, some of these sections will represent unexpected interruptions.

Because the life line is the channel for the vitality, think of it as a riverbed. Each time the channel is dug up or interrupted, the river itself must change course. This means that the river or the vitality will not have an even flow, but the fact that a new line section appears means that the flow will continue, and a new change will follow. Changes in the location of the line mean a change in the location or direction of the life itself. The broken line does not, in itself, signal bad health, unless there are markings to corroborate this.

The detour to Luna. Sometimes the life line starts on the expected route, but swings out to the Mount of Luna (Diagram H, p. 129) instead of returning in a gentle arc around the edge of the hand. In this case, the creative qualities of Luna are strong enough to pull the line to it. There is a strong desire for travel.

Line-breaking and extroversion/introversion. As Diagram C illustrated, a wide arc belongs to an extrovert, and a narrow arc indicates an introverted personality. If the line breaks off and the ends overlap (Diagram I, p. 130), a change in the personality is signaled. If the curve grows wider with the change, the person becomes more extroverted; if the arc becomes narrower, introverted tendencies are the result. As long as the two segments run side by side, ambivalence is present. The person doesn't know how to react to people and situations, and were he or she to meet the same situation twice, they would react in two different ways. There is always a pull toward introversion and extroversion for the period in which the two lines overlap. The ultimate direction of the line as it continues after the overlap indicates which tendency will be stronger.

A very deep life line adds steadiness to the personality. Its significance lies in the fact that a deep line symbolically provides a very good channel for the forces that must pass through it, and because the life line is a pivotal line, providing strength for all phases of life, a deep life line is very positive.

A light life line, one so pale that you may have to look twice to see if it is there and the course it takes, means that the person needs peace and quiet. Vitality is low and must be replenished. This person does not have the endurance that accompanies a deep life line. However, steps to increase physical strength will show up in a life line that grows deeper, just as habits that are debilitating will cause the line to become lighter.

Variation in depth. If a life line varies in depth, periods of changing health are indicated. Such variation can also mark periods when the person puts forth a great deal of effort and then stands back to take a rest.

MARKS ON THE LINES

Islands signal a splitting of energy, and on the life line they can refer to specific health problems. An island **near the first third of the line** (Diagram J, p. 130) often accompanies a congenital weakness in the spine. People with spina bifida or curvature of the spine will have these islands. Such a sign can also accompany a back injury.

An island **at the very beginning of the life line** (Diagram K, p. 130) shows an inability to concentrate early in life. People with this island often disliked school very much or had to interrupt their studies. This island has also been associated with adopted children, with people who are not sure of their origins. The island itself is a very graphic indication of dual origins. If your client has this type of island, you will have to explore the various meanings.

Chains. If the line is chained **at the beginning** (Diagram L, p. 130), this person had many childhood illnesses. A life line that stays chained **for much of its length** means a very emotional person. This person's health often suffers because there is constant turmoil or uproar. If your client has this line, offer a reminder that calmness will be a benefit in the long run. Nothing is so urgent or pressing that it should take precedence over health and peace of mind.

Dots. A deep dot at the beginning of the life line can indicate a tonsillectomy during childhood. Try out this meaning by asking clients with such a dot if they have had a tonsillectomy. In time you will come to recognize the sign clearly. The dot is deep and quite easy to spot, for it stands out from any other dots. A dot in the same area that is deep and also blue, as if a vein were crossing it, often indicates that the person has had pneumonia. Any other dots along the life line signal minor health problems. Ask your client about any particular sickness if you see these dots, taking care to look at dots you judge to belong to years already past. These are the only instances your client can verify, and you will learn with this process.

Judging time on the life line is at best an approximate process. Even so, reasonably accurate and certainly significant time spans can be seen. Time as seen in the hand is really bundled up in relative parcels, and stamping a very specific date on events past is rather more intuitive than scientific. However, a breakdown of years in terms of periods of time is possible. From this, a determination of specific years can be approximated.

Time is psychological in the sense that each of us responds to it differently, and we structure our life and efforts according to our perception of it. For this reason, it is a good idea to have a fixed starting point for the time divisions in the hand. Time in the hand is best seen in the life line.

The thirty-five-year mark. With one index finger draw an imaginary line down the middle of the Saturn finger and continue this line until it meets up with the life line (Diagram M, p. 131). This point represents thirty-five years of age. For some people, there will be a longer section of the life line above the thirty-five-year mark—and for others a longer section after that mark. The longest section signals the portion of life that is more important to the person's evolution and the development of talents. In some cases, the thirty-five-year point falls exactly at the midpoint of the life line. This means the first and second halves of the life are equally significant in the individual's development.

Once you have determined the thirty-five-year mark, take the top half of the life line and mentally divide this half into five sections. Each one of these sections will encompass seven years (Diagram N, p. 131). Divide the second half of the life line into three sections, or thirds. The first third beyond the thirty-five-year mark covers the years thirty-six to fifty; the second third refers to the fifties and sixties; and the last third to seventy and beyond.

Establishing guidelines through dialogue. As you talk with your clients and discuss the marks on their life lines, relating them to specific events at specific times, you will become adept at judging time on the life line within the guidelines just given. These guidelines are a good starting point for arriving at specific years. Only practice will help you to sharpen your ability to see time in the hand.

The timing of events is best seen in the life line. Some palmists use the heart and head lines as well to determine timing. Because of the extreme variation in the course taken by these lines, it is doubtful that there is any certain method of sectioning them. It could be said the heart and head know no time, but in the case of the life line, genetic timing, the rhythms and cycles of the body, is recorded. Thus, the timing of events suggested by the markings on the head and heart lines is best determined by checking for corroboration in the life line. Timing for specific events will be corroborated by the various markings on the life line.

Bars on the life line (Diagram O, p. 131), at any point on the line, signify problems that are irritating, momentary setbacks. Interference from others, inner attitudes, and outside events can cause these little bar lines to form. They should be discussed with your client to get at their fullest meaning.

Crosses will fall either alongside the line or right on it. When they are **right on the line,** they mean a serious or very real obstacle to health or well-being. Crosses like these come as a result of injury and accidents or severe setbacks. There is yet another meaning, though, for these setbacks can be a product of the mind only. The disturbance will either be past or current, both of which you can explore by talking to your client. If the troubles seem to be in the future, then an obstacle is being built up by mental attitudes and living habits. In either case, a discussion is called for to help you determine the meaning and appropriate advice.

Crosses outside but not touching the life line (Diagram P, p. 131), at the beginning of the life line, usually mean that the family moved when your client was young or had financial reverses.

The St. Andrew's cross. A cross at the bottom of the life line that touches both it and the fate line (Diagram Q, p. 132) is called the St. Andrew's cross. It means a potential for saving a life, either figuratively or literally. It may mean that your client has pulled someone out of the river or rescued someone from fire or other dangerous circumstances in a rather dramatic way, but more likely, it will refer to a less dramatic type of life-saving. This sign is seen on the hands of doctors, nurses, medical technicians, and pharmacists.

Breaks in the line. Any break in the line's course indicates an interruption in the current flowing through the line. The consequences of this interruption can be interpreted by what follows the break. The line may continue very strongly after the break. If you see this, and the break appears to coincide with a time already past in your client's life, ask about any major changes he or she has made. If the lines from the break overlap each other, the transition has been a smooth one.

The necessity of dialogue. By now, it is apparent just how much palmistry functions as a dialogue between you and the client. To interpret the little signs, and some of the major signs, you have to tailor the interpretations to your clients, their lives, and direction. You can only arrive at this individualized interpretation by asking questions at certain points, and such interpretation is no doubt more productive in the long run than *telling* them meanings that come to your mind for the minor signs—which will have significance, after all, only according to the life being led. No one system of personality inventory or attempt at understanding another can be laid out without incorporating the flexibility that allows for individual differences and growth—hence the wisdom of sidestepping categorical meanings in favor of a deeper understanding of the overall hand, which, in turn, culminates in an interpretation of minor signs according to the individual life and circumstances.

There are just a few more variations for the life line, and these have specific meanings.

Squares that cover any break in the life line act as a connector or container for the interrupted flow of energy. Squares soften any transition in health or changes in location or lifestyle. Traditionally, a square inside the life line was read as a sign of imprisonment—another application altogether of the square's containing force!

Rising branches on the life line show periods of ambition and efforts to better one's life.

Descending branches, usually at the bottom of the life line (Diagram R, p. 132), indicate weakening vitality. Steps to reverse this can be taken, especially if the lines appear on the hand early in life. Diet, good nutrition, and rest are helpful in clearing up these lines and remedying the low vitality.

A line inside the life line that closely parallels it (Diagram S, p. 132) serves as additional protection for the body. The inner line, sometimes called the "antibody" line, means extra physical strength and resistance to disease.

A life line ending in a fork (Diagram T, p. 132) indicates a weakening of vitality toward the end of life, but no more than we are accustomed to expect. One prong of the fork going over to the Mount of Luna reveals a desire for travel and new horizons. This desire is characteristic of the person throughout their whole life.

LIFE LINE

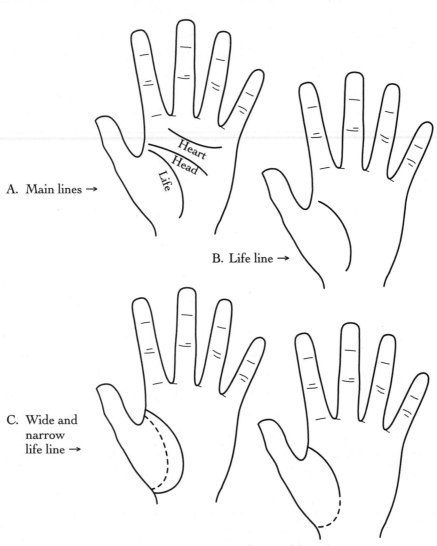

A. Main lines →

B. Life line →

C. Wide and narrow life line →

D. Short and long ↑ (dotted) life line

LIFE LINE

Line Changes Course

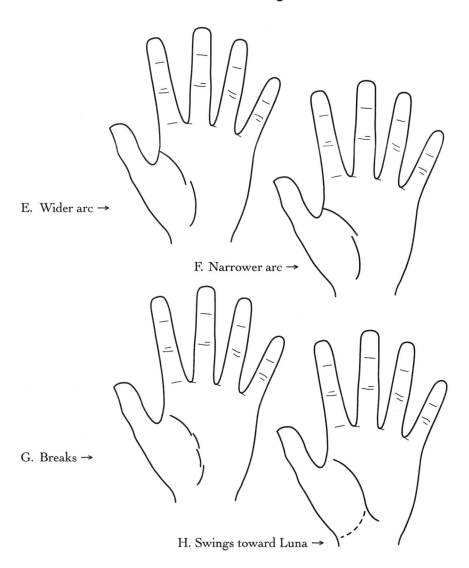

E. Wider arc →

F. Narrower arc →

G. Breaks →

H. Swings toward Luna →

LIFE LINE

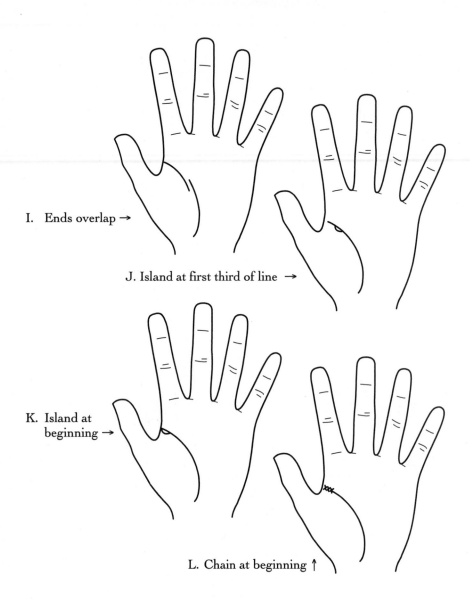

I.   Ends overlap →

J. Island at first third of line →

K. Island at
beginning →

L. Chain at beginning ↑

TIME ON LIFE LINE

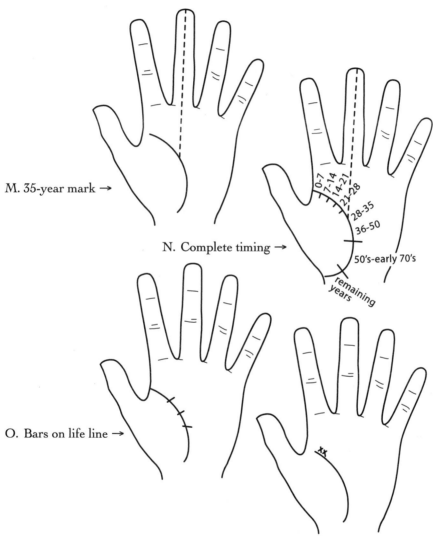

M. 35-year mark →

N. Complete timing →

0-7
7-14
14-21
21-28
28-35
36-50
50's-early 70's
remaining years

O. Bars on life line →

P. Crosses at beginning, but ↑
not touching life line

Life Line Variations

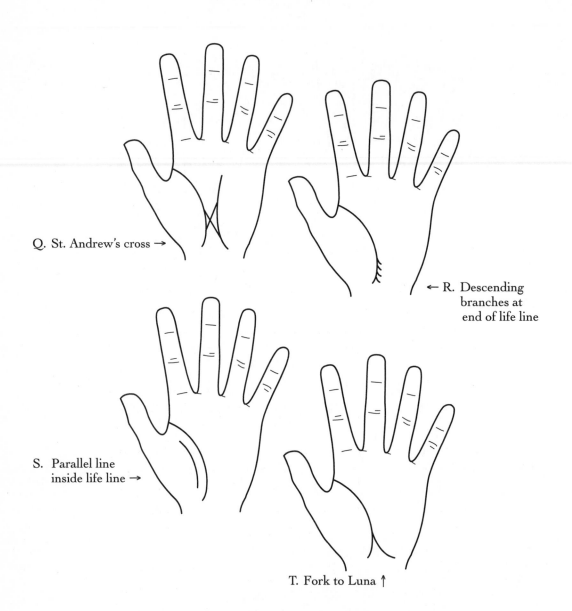

Q. St. Andrew's cross →

← R. Descending
branches at
end of life line

S. Parallel line
inside life line →

T. Fork to Luna ↑

16

The Heart Line

The heart line is indeed a love line, but it never foretells marriage. Its importance is in its role as a guide to individual emotions and their manner of expression. A study of the heart line highlights the variety of approaches to love, for the line itself takes an amazing number of forms. Some heart lines are curved, others are straight; some have branches or forks and others are a single line only. This variety in types makes an endless combination of designs.

The line begins under Mercury and usually ends on or near the Mount of Jupiter. All the categories applied to the life line also apply to the heart line: length, branches, islands, chains, crosses, dots, bars, and other signs. To analyze this line, the first thing to do, before noting the markings, is to note its length, direction, and other general characteristics, such as forking, curving, waviness, and depth. When you have taken the line's general appearance into account, you will have this basic information: the type of emotions, their depth, and their manner of expression.

Some people hold their affections in check and others express their love freely. Some need a more concrete demonstration of love than others. The people who need very much to be told or shown that they are loved usually are prepared to give the same in return, for the heart line reflects a two-way flow. It shows both the way a person is prepared to love and what he or she expects in return. One person may be more contained emotionally, and, though feelings run deep, he or she does not need to express them constantly, nor do they seek frequent emotional reassurance from others.

Understanding these approaches and tendencies on the basis of the heart line is an invaluable aid, for, as a palmist, you will receive many questions about love and will have to counsel clients on their relationships with their loved ones.

Compatibility analysis. To give an adequate analysis you need to see the hands of the people involved, to study the emotional needs portrayed in the heart line. Communication will be helped or hindered according to the degree of compatibility that exists between the partners' approaches to love. Guidance in advance can dispel areas of possible misunderstandings. The issue is not so much mismatched heart lines as the couple's willingness to understand each other's needs.

Analyzing the heart lines of each person involved in a relationship will help to highlight areas of compatibility and to point out areas that need work and understanding. Each approach to love is private and individual, but the pattern the heart line takes can help define individual needs and expectations.

LENGTH AND DIRECTION

The average heart line extends to Jupiter; some heart lines stop short on Saturn, and others end between Jupiter and the Saturn finger. The length of the line is directly proportional to the scope of expression of the affections; its direction, its termination high or low on the hand, indicates the degree to which the affections are expressed and whether the person is objective or subjective in his or her approach to love.

The typical line. When the heart line **ends under Jupiter** (Diagram A, p. 141) and has no branches, it signals a balanced approach to love. The person with such a line is steady and consistent in affections, not needing variety or outside interests.

A line that rises **high under Jupiter** (Diagram B, p. 141) is longer than normal and points to increased power. Because Jupiter is the mount concerned with authority, prestige, communication, and an enjoyment of life, a heart line rising up on this mount reflects these qualities, for the mount draws the line to itself. This type of line means a hearty and outgoing nature in love, and if the line rises to the top of this mount of authority, jealousy may become a personal characteristic. The person with this kind of heart line is dynamic in expressing affections but perhaps expects too much in return.

A heart line that **ends low on Jupiter** (Diagram C, p. 141) signifies an idealistic approach to love, and a straight heart line confirms idealism and reserve in expressing affections.

The medium short line. When the heart line ends between the index and middle fingers (Diagram D, p. 141), the client is likely to possess an affectionate nature and a strong desire for harmony. Should the line go all the way up to the top of the hand (Diagram D, dotted extension), he or she will at times go overboard in affections. The love object can do no wrong, for the person is blind to the faults of those he or she loves.

High and low heart lines. The higher the heart line ends in the hand, the greater subjectivity the person has. A more objective and detached viewpoint is possible when the heart line ends low in the hand. The low heart line indicates a better perspective but also a tendency to be critical of the loved one. A line that swings high up on the hand is apt to indicate unquestioning loyalty. The loyalty is positive but intensity should be controlled, and the person should try to be more realistic.

The short line. When the heart line ends under Saturn, the span of affections is shortened (Diagram E, p. 142). Such a line has traditionally been called the sign of a selfish approach to love. It is true that the field of action or arena of expression for the affections is smaller, but if the heart line is deep, there will be deeply felt and lively emotions. What will be missing are the outlets (shown by the extension of the heart line) for demonstrating romantic feelings and loving impulses.

As a result, most people who have a heart line ending on Saturn are marked by a very searching attitude toward love. These people are not carried away because they lack the means of expression. However, because Saturn itself indicates a search for wisdom and the process of learning through repeated experience, these qualities apply to the heart line that ends on this mount. Most everyone whose heart line ends under Saturn will be actively involved in a search for many partners in order to discover the meaning and nature of love. These people are constantly trying to define love through their loved ones. No answer seems definitive and the search goes on. These people may marry late in life. If they marry early, their partners will necessarily be involved in the learning process these persons undergo in their search for a solid definition of love. The energy turns inward for this search rather than outward in the active expression that is characteristic of those with a longer heart line.

OTHER GENERAL FEATURES

Forking at the end. Any forks on the heart line as it ends will increase the potential for expressing the self through love. **A fork under Jupiter** is considered ideal; it increases the good meaning of the line which ends in the center of Jupiter (Diagram F, p. 142). The affections are still constant, but have more variety of expression.

The Jupiter-middle finger fork. A fork that has a branch on Jupiter and another rising up between the index and middle fingers (Diagram G, p. 142) shows a strong desire for domestic harmony. People with such a fork like peaceful surroundings and especially expect their homes to be havens. They are willing to compromise and make an effort with their partner to have this peace. If something prevents peaceful surroundings, they will naturally want to retreat, and will, in most circumstances, become withdrawn.

With **a fork under Saturn** (Diagram H, p. 142), the line still retains its meaning of a search for love, but the added prong is equivalent to an outlet for the affections. A person with such a fork can search for a deeper meaning of love and simultaneously express what he or she feels.

A triple-pronged fork usually extends in the hand in such a way that one prong goes to Jupiter, one between the index and middle fingers, and one to Saturn (Diagram I, p. 143). This line indicates a dynamo of emotional power. A sense of drama accompanies the affections. All the meanings for each of the endings taken separately will be combined in this line. To learn which tendency comes more naturally to the person, look for the deepest prong. The deepest prong of the three shows the most natural or ingrained response, although the remaining prongs reflect added variety of self-expression. People with triple-pronged forks have enough emotional energy to manage homes, careers, children, and outside interests.

Branching at the beginning. Branches on the heart line as it starts under the Mount of Mercury (Diagram J, p. 143) signal a "flirt." It is easy to see why this meaning evolved, for any branch on the heart line increases the range of expression for the feelings. If the heart line starts branched, then the initial impact of acting out emotions is greater. Others are immediately aware that this person is emoting or flirting, for such wealth of expression is unusual in the very early stages of a relationship.

This richness of outer expression, this magnetism, sometimes seen as flirtatiousness, is often matched with fertility. Women with these branches at the beginning of the heart line are known to conceive children rather easily, especially if there are many branches.

The curving line. Whenever the heart line curves (Diagram K, p. 143), it shows a need to act out and express what is felt. A person with a curved heart line will be very demonstrative. Partners and loved ones usually know what is on this person's mind. He or she will be enthusiastic by nature.

The straight line. A cooler approach to love and a muted enthusiasm come more naturally to people who have straight heart lines (Diagram L, p. 143). Affections will run deep if the heart line itself has depth, but the emotional expression is contained or reserved. The straight heart line means that the person does not need a constant display of affection from others and does not readily show what he or she feels.

The wavy line (Diagram M, p. 144) belongs to someone whose emotions are not constant. This person has a great deal of growth potential, being multifaceted in self-expression, but may seem unpredictable because he or she probably would not react in the same way twice to similar situations. A wavy heart line is the mark of an intriguing person who is dissatisfied with routine.

Heart line depth. A heart line that is traced lightly in the hand shows emotions that are felt quickly but not deeply. Emotions are expressed now and forgotten later. The emotional impact of events and interaction with others is retained for quite a while if the line is deep.

Changes in depth on the heart line could refer to the heart itself. The action of the heart may be irregular. This irregularity can be confirmed only if there is a great variation in the appearance of the line. A line that grows thin at the end does not signify the same thing as a line that grows thin and then thick again as it crosses the hand. Lines always become thin as they end; this is their natural appearance.

Parallel lines. Any line that is parallel to the heart line (Diagram N, p. 144) indicates an increased range of emotional expression. People with this sign are lively and animated.

MARKINGS

Chains on the heart line (Diagram O, p. 144) mean a volatile person. Such a person is carried along on great currents of emotion and needs to cultivate quieter, calmer emotions for a better perspective.

Any **island** on the line (Diagram P, p. 144) will refer to a physical condition or to a trying emotional period. Because time cannot be measured reliably on the heart line, the palmist shouldn't focus on predicting *when* these problems will surface, unless there is strong corroboration for timing in the life line. Rather, to be constructive, the emphasis should be on ways in which the person can adjust to, or compensate for, the problems indicated—ways discovered by looking at the hand and personality as a whole, not dwelling on the problem area alone. Because it is hard to diagnose physical conditions without proper training or a medical degree, a palmist should inquire only about the emotional implications. Remember that an island shows a division of energies and indicates a feeling of confinement. The confinement could be physical or emotional; if emotional, depression is most likely meant.

If the client with an island on the heart line says that she or he has not been depressed in the past, you can carefully explore with them any current attitudes that could lead to depression later—for instance, a tendency to expect too much of others, or any perspective that needs to be aligned more closely with reality.

An island may reflect an upcoming event that is likely to be disturbing. The best prevention will still lie in developing a strong mental outlook. Inner resources are necessary if one is to combat the tendencies associated with an island on the heart line. With inner strength any difficulty can be minimized or overcome.

Small **bars** on the heart line signify trouble or obstacles to be overcome. If a person has several bars, especially under Saturn (Diagram Q, p. 145), a need for variety and a change of scene are shown. This person is restless and seeks out new adventures.

Crosses on or near the heart line represent blocks to the affections, usually in the form of outside interference.

Dots on the heart line signify surprises or shocks. The person with a dotted heart line has heard unexpected news at some point in life. This news was of major import and deeply affected her or him, or those close to them.

A dot can be recognized as an indentation that looks as if a pencil point or needle has poked a tiny hole in the line. The impression or indentation remains. These indentations interrupt the flow of the energy represented by the heart line and may mean that the person leads too stimulating a life. The lifestyle takes its toll on the body. If you see these dots on a client's hand, and your client cannot remember receiving any surprising news, then explore with him or her the pace of their life and activities. They may need to slow down to stay in the best of health.

The broken line. Another clue to health, indicating a problem that needs guarding against, is seen in the broken heart line, especially a line broken in more than one place (Diagram R, p. 145). These breaks show an interruption in the energy flow and a lessening of physical and emotional vitality. Many times this line is formed after a trauma that substantially alters a person's outlook and lifestyle.

Descending branches on the heart line (Diagram S, p. 145) sometimes show disappointment over the way a certain project or love affair turned out. The lines droop much as spirits fall during a breakup with a loved one.

These descending branches have another meaning, however. If there are many of them, across the entire heart line, it means that the power of the head line draws these lines to itself. In effect, the head controls the heart. A whole series of descending lines means that this tendency for the head to rule the heart is inborn, but one or two lines dropping toward the head line refer to specific instances when the head ruled the heart.

Rising branch lines on the heart line indicate buoyant spirits. The person is optimistic, with overflowing energy and emotions. He or she is cheerful and open to new experiences.

Any **square** on the heart line symbolizes protection from physical or emotional difficulty.

In summary, in order to grasp the full significance of the heart line, a palmist needs to consider all the following:

- How long is the heart line?
- Does the line have branches?
- Does it fork?
- Is the line curved or straight?

- Is the line light or deep?
- What are the various markings?

Once you have established the length of the line and the course it takes, you can concentrate on all the markings. More than any other major line, the heart line is likely to have numerous branches and marks. This is not surprising, for expression of the heart is as creative and infinite as the potential of life itself.

HEART LINE

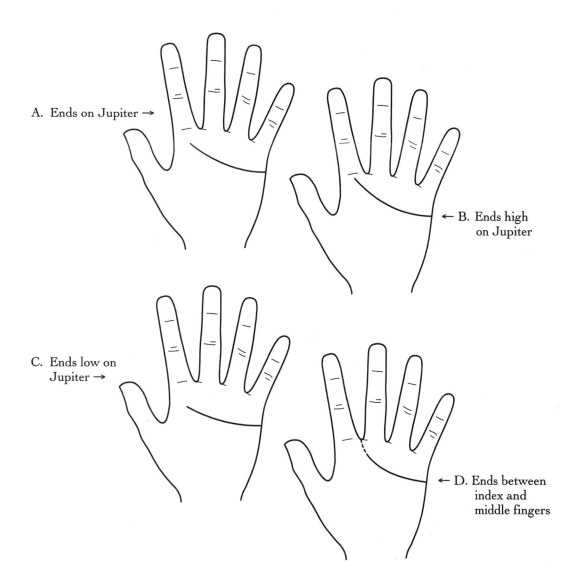

A. Ends on Jupiter →

← B. Ends high
on Jupiter

C. Ends low on
Jupiter →

← D. Ends between
index and
middle fingers

HEART LINE

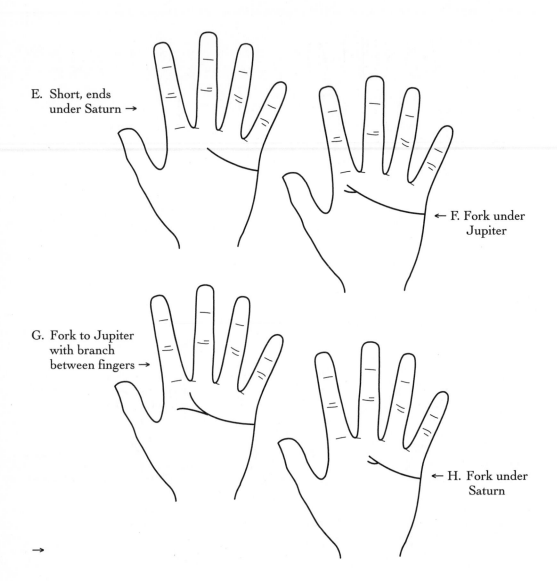

E. Short, ends
   under Saturn →

← F. Fork under
   Jupiter

G. Fork to Jupiter
   with branch
   between fingers →

← H. Fork under
   Saturn

→

HEART LINE

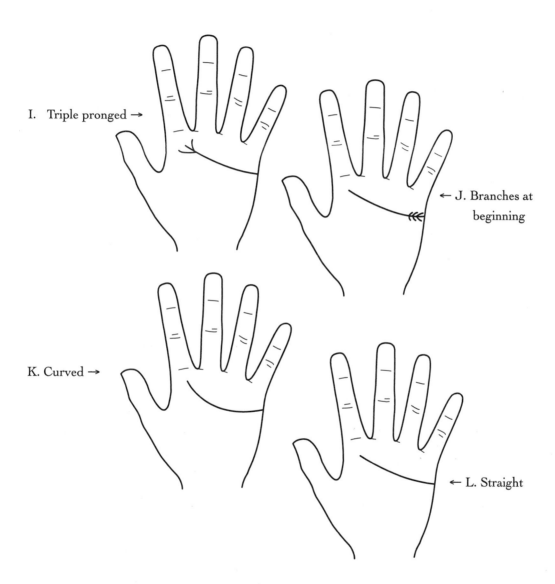

I.   Triple pronged →

← J. Branches at
beginning

K. Curved →

← L. Straight

HEART LINE

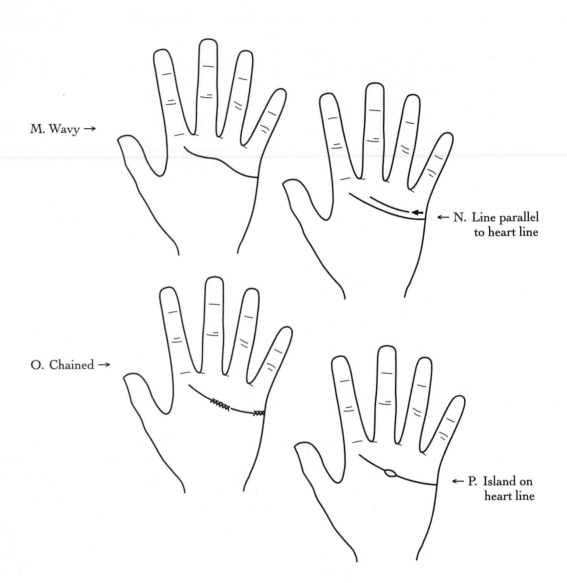

M. Wavy →

← N. Line parallel
   to heart line

O. Chained →

← P. Island on
   heart line

HEART LINE

Q. Bars

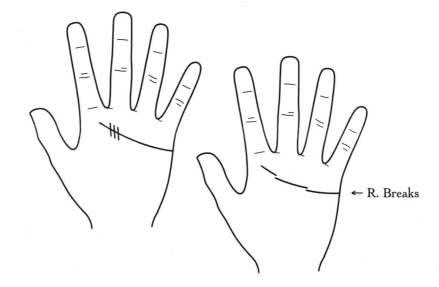

← R. Breaks

S. Descending branches →

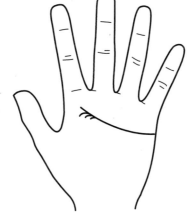

17

The Head Line

The head line has to be examined for length and depth, which show the scope of mental interests and curiosity, and the mental outlook; for its course, which reveals how imaginative and independent the person is; and for forks and markings, which add specific meanings to the line.

Just as there are many different types of mentalities and approaches to life dictated by the mind, there are several configurations for the beginning and ending of the line.

The head line begins under the Jupiter finger. It has six possible starting points: inside the life line, just touching the life line, tied to the life line for a certain length, just above the life line, widely separated from the life line, and stemming from the Mount of Jupiter itself.

The head line may end under the Mount of Apollo or under Mercury. In addition, the line may be straight, and consequently end on a level with the Upper Mars mount, or it may dip slightly below this mount. It may also take a strong curve downward and end on the Luna mount itself.

LENGTH AND DEPTH

Length. A head line is considered long if it extends beyond the Apollo mount; short, if it ends abruptly at the Saturn mount.

Short head lines signify a good memory. They also show good powers of concentration. The main meaning of a short line is the need to apply what is learned. People with these head lines like theory insofar as it is useful and has practical application. A short head line shows a single-track mind and a tendency toward specialized knowledge. Take, as an example, a small child fascinated by light bulbs and electrical wiring. No matter how much he or she is told to leave these things alone, they are irresistible. Their interest continues all through their teens, and the knowledge acquired in school is directed toward increasing their ability to work with electrical appliances. The child will grow up to become an electrician.

Long head lines are found on people whose range of interests is quite wide. The longer the line, the greater the area of probing and intellectual speculation. People with long head lines appreciate new theories for their own sake, and these people make good researchers in any field. Long head lines signal many interests and a tendency to have more than one hobby.

The length of the head line in no way indicates the amount of intelligence, but rather the direction taken by a person's understanding and their ability to learn. The difference between long and short head lines lies in the scope of application. Those with short head lines easily apply what they learn, while their counterparts are too busy absorbing information to apply all they know. Genius is possible with both types of lines, for other signs in the hands are necessary to support the delineation of genius. Outstanding signs in the fingers and their shape, a dynamic heart line, and well-developed mounts support the possibility of genius and its application in any chosen field of activity.

Depth. The head line also shows the ability to concentrate. **The deeper the head line,** the greater the ability to concentrate. With a deep head line, the person will easily finish what was started, especially if the line is straight.

A light or pale head line has an altogether different indication. It shows that the channel for mental energy is weak. Hence the person tires easily and can be subject to strain. A light head line always means that the person needs more sleep than the average person.

If your clients have light head lines, no matter what the length, tell them they need more sleep than the average, and they are likely to agree. Parents whose children have light head lines should make sure that their children get enough rest.

Changes in depth. When the head line changes in depth, so that one section lies deep in the hand while another is faint, periods of serious effort at mental growth and study and periods of rest or lack of concentrated effort to learn are indicated. Just as with the heart line, the palmist should not try to assign a date to the periods unless there is strong corroboration in the life line. The focus should be on handling the problems and realizing the potential suggested by the line. A line with this kind of variation means that the person won't be consistent in efforts to grow, but even with the lighter sections there is potential for more growth because a deeper section follows.

Noting this variation can be useful in counseling students who don't seem able to keep up their grades or adults who can't stick to one job. Once these persons realize that their hands show a tendency to "goof off" and compensate later with an effort that is too much for them, thus setting up a vicious circle of uneven attempts to achieve, they can take steps to correct these tendencies.

The Course of the Line

A wavy head line (Diagram A, p. 154) shows a mind that is easily distracted. A student having this sign surely won't listen in class and will have to rely on books later.

The straight line. The head line may be straight or curved. A head line which stays straight in its course and heads toward the Mars mount (Diagram B, p. 154) has always been said to show a practical outlook and common sense.

This inference is logical enough, for a straight line stays closer to the active zone of the hand. In this way, the mental powers are expressed in activity that is direct and to the point. Mental powers will be applied to tangible tasks by those with straight head lines.

The curved line. If the head line dips slightly below the Mount of Mars (Diagram C, p. 154), it will be curved. Such a curve signifies creativity. It also means that the person doesn't think along conventional or superficial lines. There is always a pull to dig deep into the meaning of what is learned.

The curve to Luna. If the head line continues downward, touching Luna (Diagram C, dotted extension), it shows emotional thoughts and a concern for symbols, for the line enters the unconscious zone. If the line goes directly to Luna, with a steep curve, the desire to expand mentally and to create is as large as the unconscious itself. People whose head lines veer sharply toward Luna are not easy to understand, and they often are aware of their own complexity.

The line's beginning. Where the line begins, as well as the direction it takes as it crosses the palm, is part of its general configuration. The beginning has some bearing on a person's dependence or independence. Although there are many variations possible with the beginning of the head line, the essential difference between them is a sense of caution versus impulse.

Widely separated head and life lines. A head line that is widely separated from the life line (Diagram D, p. 154)—which represents personal resources at the deepest level—means that the person is very impulsive, preferring to act and then think later. There is creativity and a joyous response to life. There may also be carelessness, but that could be balanced by other signs in the hand.

Narrowly separated lines. When the head line is just slightly separated from the life line (Diagram E, p. 155), the person will be self-confident in most of his or her responses to others, having the ability to think for him- or herself.

Touching lines. If the head line just touches the life line (Diagram F, p. 155), there is a good balance between caution and impulse. This person thinks and acts carefully, but is not inhibited.

Chained lines. The head line that starts out tied to the life line and has a chained appearance (Diagram G, p. 155) shows timidity. A person with such a line was very shy as a child. If your client is a child, do what you can to encourage his or her self-confidence. At the point where the head line separates from the life line, the shyness is overcome.

Head line inside life line. If the head line begins inside the life line (Diagram H, p. 155), the person will be defensive. Similar to the ostrich who sticks its head in the sand, the person will feel a need for protection and shelter, but will not act out this need wisely. He or she will be all the more vulnerable because of this defensiveness, thus, like the body of the ostrich above the sand, open to attack. At times the person will become belligerent in direct proportion to inner fears or nervousness, thus further increasing vulnerability to attack. Much energy is spent in marshaling defenses. This person will have to recognize and accept this tendency and be re-educated in order to conserve energy that could be spent better in other endeavors.

A trauma early in life is often associated with the head line inside the life line. Since that trauma often jolts the process of growing up in many ways, this line also is found on certain kinds of precocious children, especially on those who had to assume responsibilities early in life.

Head line starting on Jupiter. Very rarely does the head line start on Jupiter itself (Diagram I, p. 156). Such a start indicates increased personal ambition, and the person will no doubt go far in life, all other signs being equal.

FORKING AND MARKING

A fork at the end of the head line increases the mental powers, for it adds another channel for the mental energy.

There are several forms and positions for forks on the head line, and each one signifies a different talent.

"The lawyer's line." If the head line points toward Upper Mars and is high in the hand with a forked ending (Diagram J, p. 156), it is called a lawyer's head line. It shows the ability to see both sides of a question and the ability to be practical, not to get carried away until all the facts have been found. Such a fork indicates a natural talent for investigative work.

"The writer's fork." If one prong of the fork points toward Upper Mars and the other, longer prong heads toward Luna, this is the writer's fork (Diagram K, p. 156). The prong on Luna heightens the activity of the unconscious, and the prong near Mars, closer to the active zone of the hand, makes it easy to apply what the unconscious reveals.

In addition, this fork means inventive ability. It also signifies the ability to juggle the facts, and it may show a need for caution and care in remaining as honest as possible, but the main significance of this fork is writing ability, and it would be wise to counsel your client accordingly. Your client may be surprised and say he or she has never tried writing. You can assure them that if they take it up, they could be successful. If this fork is absent, the reverse is not indicated. The fork is not absolutely essential as a sign of a writer. Simply, if it is present, then there is writing ability.

A three-pronged fork at the end of the head line is rare, but, when found, it signifies extraordinary mental ability.

The branch toward Mercury. Often, a head line will have a branch going toward Mercury (Diagram L, p. 156); this reveals a concern for finances. This person has had to manage money carefully and is aware of its value. If this sign has always been on the hand or if it is as deep as the rest of the head line, it can be interpreted as a native ability to manage money, but the fact that it is a branch, and often lighter than the rest of the head line, means that money management is an acquired ability. People with this branch are very conscious of the money they spend and can monitor their finances, no matter what their scale of living.

Markings, like forking, involve specific meanings to be added to the general implications derived from the overall configuration of the head line.

Dots on the head line, especially at the beginning, and under Saturn, show either a tendency to have headaches or a need for glasses.

Crosses touching the head line (Diagram M, p. 157) traditionally mean an injury to the head, and often this is exactly what has happened. This may have resulted from a childhood accident or a sports injury.

An island along the head line signals nervous tension or strain that lasts as long as the island itself. If the island is as wide as one of the fingers (Diagram N, p. 157), the tension is prolonged. If your client has this sign, you will know he or she is under strain or likely to be in the future, and you will want to advise them of this. Maybe your attention will help them to be more aware and in control of tendencies toward overexertion.

Bars signal a hindrance of the power of the line, and if they occur early on the line, they may show an interruption in education or an unexpected change in careers. Perhaps the person got a degree in one field, only to have to enter another career area. Bars on the line near its end refer to attitudes that block complete use of personal potential. These blocks can be dispelled with effort, however, and a new direction or perspective can be achieved. Take care not to confuse segments of the Mercury line (chapter nineteen) with bars at the end of the head line.

Squares that touch or encompass the head line mean prevention of possible injury or mental strain (Diagram O, p. 157). They are a good sign.

Because there is so much to grasp to get a good understanding of the head line, it is useful to have a mental checklist. Try to make sure you have looked at all these signs:

- Length and depth of the line.
- The course it takes (wavy, curved, or straight).
- Its beginning.
- Forks and any special endings.
- Any special marks.

After examining these signs, you will have a complete reading for the head line.

HEAD LINE

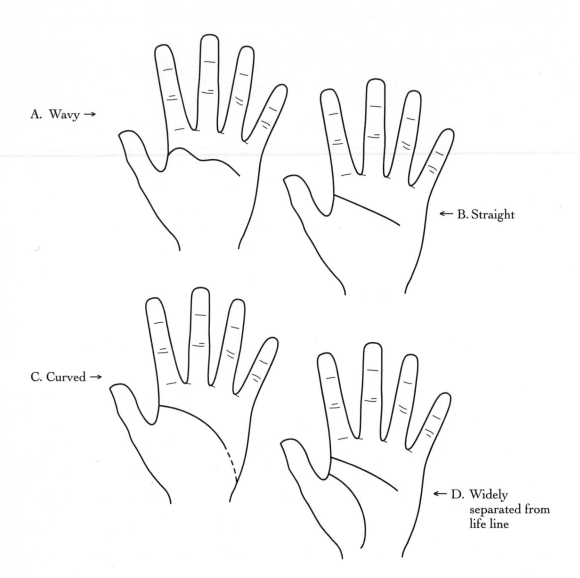

A. Wavy →

← B. Straight

C. Curved →

← D. Widely
separated from
life line

HEAD LINE

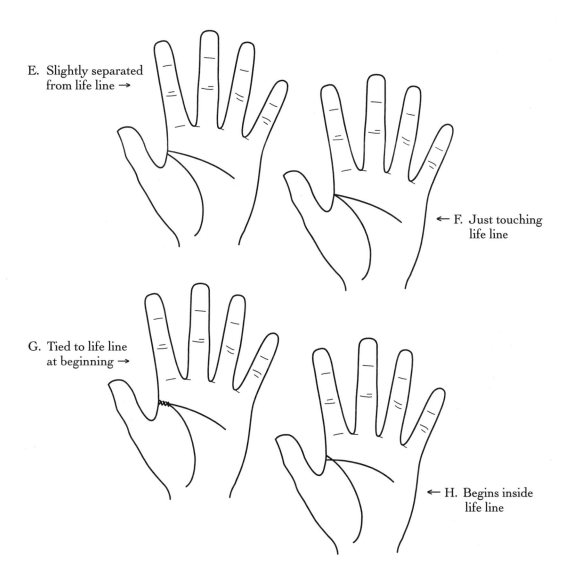

E. Slightly separated
   from life line →

← F. Just touching
   life line

G. Tied to life line
   at beginning →

← H. Begins inside
   life line

HEAD LINE

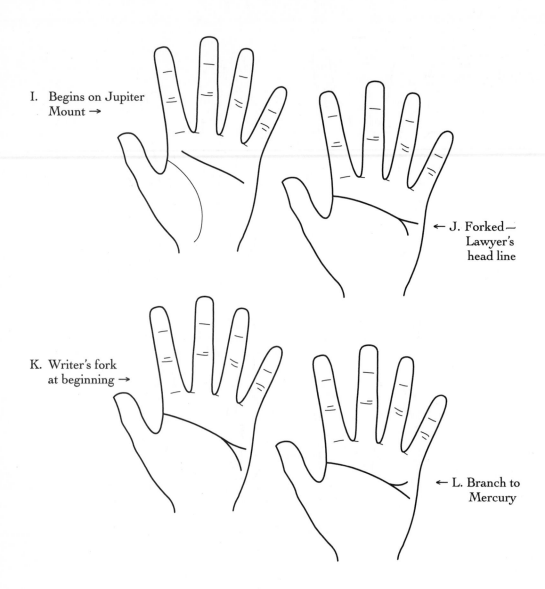

I. Begins on Jupiter
    Mount →

← J. Forked—
    Lawyer's
    head line

K. Writer's fork
    at beginning →

← L. Branch to
    Mercury

HEAD LINE

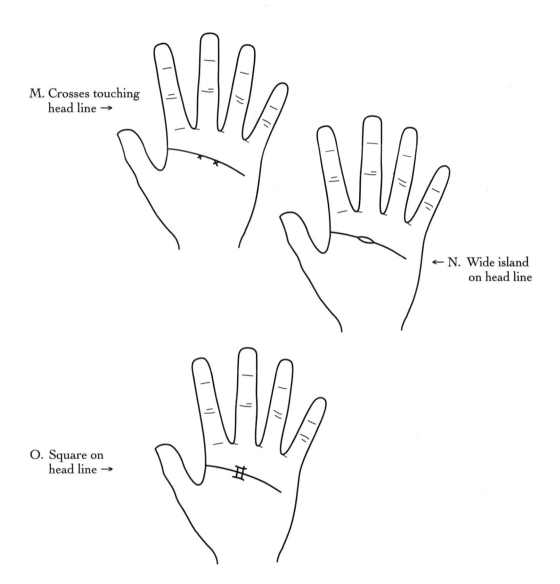

M. Crosses touching
head line →

← N. Wide island
on head line

O. Square on
head line →

18

The Fate Line

*T*he vertical line that runs under the Saturn finger is called the fate line. This name might sound misleading at first glance, for the trend today is toward de-emphasizing destiny's powers. The name, however, is appropriate, for the line reveals inner attitudes and the resulting drive or lack of drive for achievement. It is the inner attitudes, over which the person has control, that shape events, and the pattern of these events, in turn, comprises the person's fate.

Another name for this vertical line is the "line of integration." This fits very well with the definition of Saturn as a point where the conscious and unconscious forces must meet and integrate.

A vertical line has power or a positive meaning in itself, for it is a natural channel for the flow of energy between the active and passive zones of the hand, and, interestingly enough, traditional meanings for the fate line mirror the concepts contained in the zones of the hand. When the line begins low in the hand, in the passive zone, it indicates ambitions formulated in childhood. The child is not as able as an adult to act out plans for the future. He or she is limited—

hence the expression of ambitions and goals isn't as active. When the line continues up into the active zone, toward the top of the hand, more freedom of expression is possible.

The fate line may take many forms, but the presence of this line at any point in the hand shows a desire to realize certain goals and the *ability* to work for them. It also reflects integrating forces and a desire for balance that is reflected in the person's philosophy of life. It reveals the following:

- Individual sense of worth and dignity.
- The ability and inclination to work.
- A desire for results and achievements.
- A strong philosophy of life.

Starting Low or High

A low start. When the fate line starts low in the hand (Diagram A, p. 164), it shows that the person set goals early in life. This was the child who always had an answer when asked, "What do you want to be when you grow up?" Whatever the child answered may or may not have come true, but the very mention of a goal shows that he or she was thinking in terms of interacting with others. The fate line low in the hand shows well-developed social instincts.

Only in the bottom. If this line appears only in the bottom portion of the hand, the early desire to be productive was not carried over into adult life.

When the line continues upward in the hand, it suggests increased possibilities of career, marriage, and contributions to society.

To the head line. When the fate line goes just to the head line and stops (Diagram B, p. 164), it shows that no new effort is made after the age of thirty or so. The person has chosen career, partner, perhaps has had children, and has pretty well set a direction in life.

Shifting past the head line. If the fate line continues after this point, but shifts a little in its course (Diagram C, p. 164), it indicates a new start. A change in career or a new marriage are possible. If the line grows deeper after the head line or if another smaller line parallels it (Diagram D, p. 164), yet another dimension is added to the career already established. Possibly the person works at two different jobs. The double fate line points to a versatile person.

Past the heart line. If the fate line continues up to the heart line and past it, success in a chosen field is nearly guaranteed, for the line's extension throughout the length of the palm signals untiring effort to achieve the goals that have been set.

Starting high. Perhaps the fate line doesn't start until somewhat higher in the hand. If it first appears somewhat **below the head line** (Diagram E, p. 165), it means that a career was chosen that stimulated ambition and drive not previously there. If the fate line starts **at the head line** (Diagram F, p. 165), the career itself began in earnest when the person was nearly thirty. Achievement occurs in the mid-thirties, when the fate line starts some distance **above the head line** (Diagram G, p. 165). When it starts on or **above the heart line**, self-expression comes very late in life.

If it starts this high in the palm, the person should be encouraged to work harder at self-discovery and mastery of a skill, for the line is a promise of fulfillment that could be made to happen a little sooner—with the proper effort!

No fate line at all on the hand shows an asocial character, or a person whose norms and values are not those commonly accepted. The hand will have to be studied for other signs of ambition, desire for contact with others, and the particular talents seen in the mount development.

THE COURSE OF THE FATE LINE

The course of the fate line is determined by any one of three possible starting points: from the life line, from Luna, or from the center of the hand (Diagram H, p. 165).

From Luna. Whenever the fate line stems from the Mount of Luna, the person will achieve a substantial part of success due to the approval of others. Such a start signals a pleasing personality and an ability to work with groups of people. Sometimes it indicates people in the public eye.

From the center. If the fate line begins in the center of the hand, a sense of independence is assured. Whatever is achieved results from the person's own efforts.

From the life line. A fate line that springs from the life line and proceeds in the direction of the Saturn finger shows strong family and home ties. A person with such a line will achieve certain goals as a result of family help and interest. Often this line marks a career that others in the family have taken up also, or entrance into a family business.

MARKINGS

The same markings that apply to the other major lines can also be found on the fate line. **Islands** on the fate line show a setback in plans and goals. The islands represent trying periods, a time when the person feels trapped by circumstances.

Timing events. The fate line is the only line other than the life line for which timing can be established with any degree of certainty.

- Divide the area from the bottom of the hand to the head line into three sections: the bottom third represents the first twelve years of life, the middle section refers to the ages of approximately twelve to twenty-four, while the last section indicates the ages twenty-five through the early thirties.

- The area between the head and heart lines refers to the early thirties through the late forties.

- The area between the heart line and the top of the palm shows the late forties and up.

With this system, you can try to time the events shown by the minor signs.

Bars on the fate line mean obstacles that have to be overcome. The obstacles are interruptions from the outside, and they may impact the career or other goals, or alter the philosophy of life that once worked for the person. The bars should not be read as complete blocks to plans and goals, but as temporary hurdles.

Dots on the fate line are rare, but if there, they show sudden interruptions in plans. Dots are usually confined to the other main lines.

Chained fate lines are also very rare, but the general meaning of "confusion" can be applied to goals and plans. Once the chain disappears, goals and perspectives are clear again.

Crosses on the fate line indicate more severe or far-reaching effects. They refer to specific (and probably memorable) events that can be discussed with your client in order to arrive at the full import.

Squares signify protection, and this meaning applies to the formulation of goals and plans, as seen through the fate line. Any disruptions may be avoided through ingenuity and quick thinking.

Breaks in the fate line (Diagram I, p. 166) signal a change of course in goals, education, or other endeavors. A break usually signifies also the new outlook that follows this change. This is especially true if the line shifts course after the break. Any transition will be smooth if the ends overlap (Diagram J, p. 166).

A completely **double fate line** (Diagram K, p. 166) is the sign of a complex person. Integration of the personality and goals can be difficult, for two lines serve to emphasize the autonomy of the two sides of the hand, conscious and unconscious. Normally, these two forces symbolically meet and are gathered together in one line, even if the line is marked or changes course.

Accompanying lines. Sometimes a shorter line accompanies the fate line (Diagram L, p. 166). This lends support to the person's efforts. Two lines running parallel (Diagram M, p. 167) to a fate line that extends above the head line show a diversity of interests.

Influence lines. Short lines that come in from Luna and join the fate line (Diagram N, p. 167) are called "influence lines." They show the influence of others on the course of the person's life. Traditionally, these lines are interpreted to mean the possibility of marriage or a long-term partnership.

A wavy fate line (Diagram O, p. 167) points to indecision in choosing values and a fluctuating philosophy and outlook on life. A person with such a line can be swayed by what others say and do, and perhaps looks to the wrong sources for guidance.

Changing depth. A line that is deep and grows fainter, only to become deep again, indicates an uneven effort to reach personal goals. At times the person burrows into intense efforts and at other times reduces the effort, sliding along for a while, perhaps in order to get a better view and renewed perspective for the things he or she is doing.

Whatever type of perspective is embraced by the person, the fate line denotes the necessary ambition to carry out goals. It also reflects relationships, and its starting point tells how one is likely to react to others: a Luna starting point means that the person will look to the outside for help and support; starting in the center of the hand means that the attitude will be individualistic; and starting at the life line points to a need for family closeness.

These relationships, along with the power and desire to grow, will shape the person's life.

FATE LINE

A. Starts low in hand →

← B. Stops at head line

C. Shifts position after →
crossing head line

← D. Becomes two
parallel lines
after head line

FATE LINE

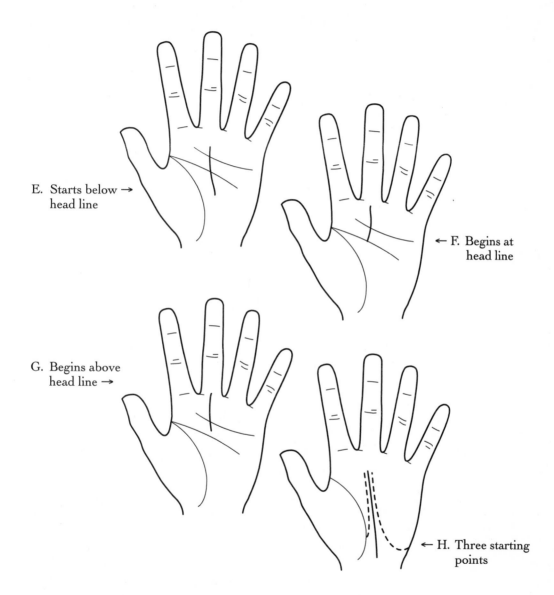

E. Starts below → head line

← F. Begins at head line

G. Begins above head line →

← H. Three starting points

FATE LINE

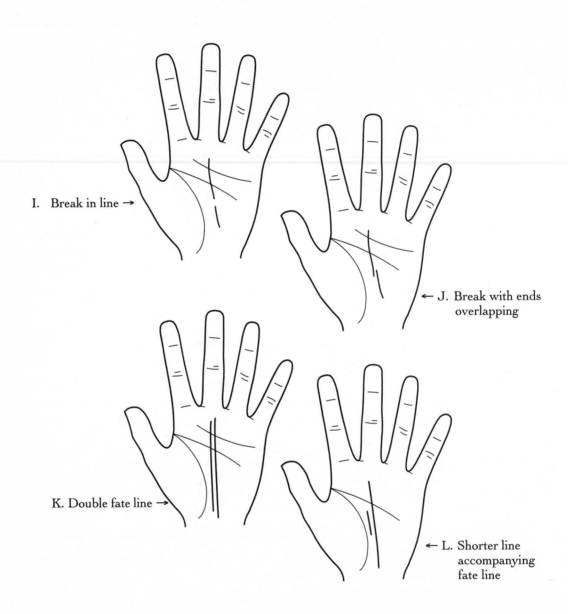

I. Break in line →

← J. Break with ends
       overlapping

K. Double fate line →

← L. Shorter line
       accompanying
       fate line

FATE LINE

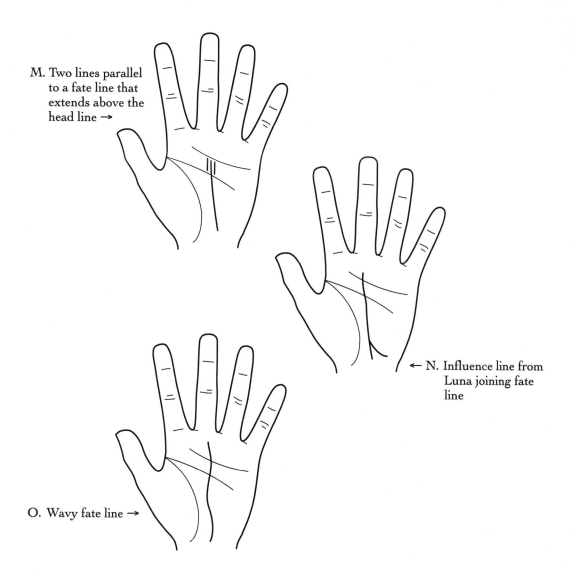

M. Two lines parallel
to a fate line that
extends above the
head line →

← N. Influence line from
Luna joining fate
line

O. Wavy fate line →

19

❦

The Apollo and Mercury Lines

*B*oth of these lines highlight the creativity of a person by accenting the unconscious and providing a vehicle for its expression. Both lines lie mainly in the unconscious section of the hand, and they are vertical lines, which signal rising power.

THE APOLLO LINE

The Apollo line (Diagram A, p. 174) is the first vertical line to fall entirely in the unconscious half of the hand. Its position means that quite a bit of energy from the unconscious is available to the personality. The Apollo line represents a channel for any creative self-expression and development of talent.

This line follows a very definite course in that it will only end directly under the Mount of Apollo if it is a true Apollo line. The line may not reach clear to the top of the hand, but the eye can tell if it is aligned with the Apollo mount when it is present lower in the hand.

The line can start at any of several points in the hand, but the longer the line, the more power is expressed. This line was once called a lucky line and was interpreted to promise fame and riches. The only certain wealth associated with this line is an inner wealth. The line is lucky insofar as it signals above-average talent. It must be backed by a good fate line to produce results.

The Apollo line means an ability to use the rich life of the unconscious in a way that corresponds to the qualities of the Apollo mount: creativity, musicality, artistic or humanistic endeavors.

At times, success does seem to happen without effort. In this case luck is usually a legacy, interior or monetary, shown by two lines on either side of the Apollo line (Diagram B, p. 174).

Starting low. Those with a line starting low in the hand and continuing to the Apollo mount have more than enough talent to produce results. These are people to watch!

Starting at Luna. The line may start from the general direction of Luna before it comes to roost under the Apollo mount, indicating public acceptance of the person's talents.

Centered under Apollo. A line centered under Apollo stresses individual efforts, but any sway toward the life line at the beginning of the Apollo line indicates family influence. Perhaps the talent is inherited.

Starting after the head line. If the line begins after the head line, many years will be needed to polish and market the indicated talent. Traditionally, this type of line means success that comes later in life.

Two or more Apollo lines above the heart line signal several interests, all of which call for attention. The person will want to display his or her versatility, and will be most at home working on a number of interesting projects. The only drawback associated with this sign is a tendency to become scattered and a failure to accomplish anything solid while pursuing any one of a multitude of interests.

Depth. The deeper the line, the more marked are the qualities associated with Apollo: creativity, self-expression, and a desire to be in the public eye.

A light Apollo line means that the person is at least aware of having creative ability, but is timid in doing anything with it. He or she needs some encouragement. Taking the time and mustering the courage necessary for completing one project would help this person immensely. A single success could bolster and prod her or him on to bigger and better things. The potential is always there if the Apollo line is present.

Islands on the Apollo line mark a time when creative powers are at a low ebb. The person will feel confined. Traditionally, islands in the Apollo line meant trouble with one's reputation. This is a possible interpretation, but not the only one.

A bar signifies an obstacle to creativity. Perhaps others don't understand what the person is doing.

Dots indicate a temporary interruption and some worries about the public side of the career.

Chained Apollo lines are rare, but such a sign would signal a "muddying" of the powers of self-expression for as long as the chain lasted. Positive steps would have to be taken to further creative efforts and to reach a new self-expression.

A cross on or alongside the Apollo line represents specific interference in the attempts to be artistic or creative. These blocks to creativity have to be recognized for what they are and gotten rid of.

Breaks in the line show that a new direction will be taken. A change in careers is possible.

Any square signals personal ingenuity and cleverness of a type that will protect one from mishaps.

All of the signs on an Apollo line will help to define the type of self-expression that is possible. The presence of this line alone is not enough to promise success, but it does point to an unusual personality with a flair that is above average.

THE MERCURY LINE

The Mercury line doesn't have as many variations in appearance as the other lines. The only possible variations are in the length and markings, for there is only one course the line can take: a diagonal route from the direction of the life line, extending to the Mount of Mercury (Diagram C, p. 174).

Not everyone has a Mercury line, but, when present, it shows an above-average awareness of the nervous system. Mercury lines belong to people who are very aware of internal changes in their bodies and in their state of health.

It can be illustrated this way: when a person without a Mercury line complains of feeling low, he or she won't in many cases be able to explain why or define the feeling, but if a person with a Mercury line claims to feel sick, he or she will be able to inform the world in great detail of every fluctuation in health: "at 8:00 AM I had a headache, by noon I was nauseated."

The broken line. If the Mercury line is clear and unbroken, the health is good. But little fragments or marks which break the continuity of the line show nervousness and susceptibility to sickness.

When the line points to a nervous person, the symptoms of nervousness are likely to be expressed through an upset stomach, especially if the Mercury line is broken or made up of several sections (Diagram D, p. 174).

An island on the Mercury line, especially at the point where it crosses the head line (Diagram E, p. 175), shows a weakness of the lungs or bronchial tubes. As a palmist, you should ask if your clients smoke, and if the answer is "yes," you can warn them that anything that might weaken the lungs or respiratory system certainly isn't advisable in their case!

Business ability. A good, strong Mercury line has been associated with business ability. This is logical for two reasons. The Mercury mount itself can mean business ability, and the line appears under this mount, thus sharing its qualities. Secondly, a healthy nervous system is indicated by a good Mercury line, a temperament that can take the pressures of competition and the business world.

If your client doesn't have a Mercury line, this in no way cancels a talent for business. Other signs, along with a good Mount of Mercury, may point to this ability. The absence of the Mercury line promises a quiet or calm nervous system.

Hunches and occult ability. If the nervous system is especially active, as indicated by the line itself, additional meanings of a talent for accurate hunches and occult ability might apply. Again, these meanings derive from the line's association with the Mercury mount and its characteristics.

The "intuition crescent." There is another line that is a true intuition line (Diagram F, p. 175). This line is a crescent on the unconscious part of the hand, extending from Upper Mars to Luna. When this line is well developed, psychic powers are undeniable. If your client has this sign, be sure to ask about their psychic adventures.

Horizontal lines on the Mercury mount. One area under Mercury itself remains to be treated: the small horizontal lines on the outside edge of the mount and any smaller lines that are perpendicular to them (Diagram G, p. 175). The horizontal lines, or a single horizontal line, signal the ability to be involved in relationships with others, a knowledge of the give and take that is necessary for partnerships. If there is more than one line present, there is an above-average capacity for love. Such a sign may indicate more than one marriage. However, no line is a legal sign in itself, and the marriage(s) may or may not be sealed and witnessed by state or church procedures. It simply isn't possible to predict a certain number of marriages by these lines. At their best, they show a very loving person, and a person who is willing to be involved with others. These qualities increase chances for matrimony indeed.

Perpendicular lines. Lines perpendicular to the horizontal lines refer to an interest in children. If there are two or more of these lines, the individual is very disposed to have or care for children. The lines don't promise parenthood in the physical sense, but they always highlight an interest in and affinity for children.

This information in itself is sufficient to counsel every client who wants to know what form her or his love life will take. Each of these lines, horizontal and vertical, signal preparation for the responsibilities of loving another person.

Together, the Apollo and Mercury lines denote another source of power. They are the expression of creative impulses that would otherwise remain stifled or unheeded. These two lines show a sensitive person, a person who is very aware of him- or herself and their interaction with others and the environment. This awareness leads to infinite possibilities for an expanded and interesting life. When a person has both of these lines, he or she will experience variety in life, both in friendships and experiences.

A. Apollo line →

← B. Legacy lines

C. Mercury line →

← D. Fragmented
Mercury line

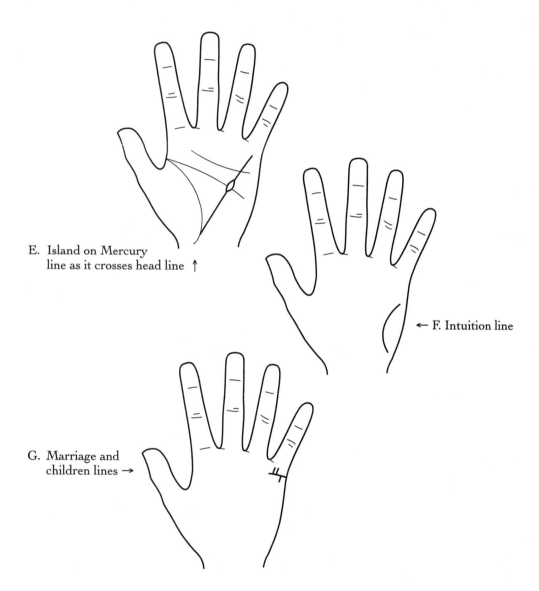

E. Island on Mercury
    line as it crosses head line ↑

← F. Intuition line

G. Marriage and
    children lines →

20

Interpreting the Whole Hand

So far we have looked at the meaning of each of the individual traits of the hand. However, throughout we have stressed that each trait must be viewed in terms of the whole hand. The palmist must be able to grasp the unique interplay of the various traits that come to light in a thorough analysis of the hands.

To be thorough, an analysis does not necessarily have to be long or detailed. A thorough reading is best achieved by an analysis that takes into account any and all opposing or dissimilar traits associated with the interpretations of specific areas of the hand.

This approach to hand analysis is so important that a few samples of a synthesis of conflicting traits are given here as examples. It is vital to remember that no single trait stands alone. Each and every trait is modified by the import of all the traits taken together.

- Head line tied to the life line at the beginning.
- Heart line curves.

- Life line breaks, the ends overlap and the new segment of the line continues in a wider arc.

Initial shyness and timidity as a child, demonstrated by the beginning of the head line, has an excellent chance of being overcome. The curving heart line shows an outgoing, affectionate nature. The later shift in the life line further adds to the potential for a more outgoing nature, for the wider arc taken by the new segment of the line points to increased vital forces in the personality.

- All lines in the hand deeply etched.
- Mounts flat, hand firm.
- Thin, waisted thumb.

The depth of the lines indicates very strong natural vitality and endurance, while firm, flat mounts suggest stamina. People with this hand can be very persistent and single-minded in the expenditure of energy to achieve their goals. However, a thin, waisted thumb signals tact and consideration in the personality that make these persons thoughtful and rather delicate in their approach to others.

- Forked heart line: one branch goes to the Jupiter mount, the other between the index and middle fingers.
- Straight head line.
- Well-developed lower Mars mount.

The heart line shows a desire for domestic harmony and tranquility. The straight head line supports this clue, for it suggests a person who is self-possessed and balanced in his or her outlook on life. His or her expectations of others are reasonable, but the highly developed lower Mars mount points to a person who can become impatient and irritable. In this case, initiative and ambition, also associated with this mount, will be channeled into realistic projects, projects that have a good chance of succeeding because this person has stamina and endurance, as shown by the straight head line, and the realistic outlook reflected in the heart line.

Signs from the back of the hands can be analyzed in the same fashion:

- Hands flat on tabletop, fingers spread wide apart.
- Nails pale and narrow.
- Bulges at the knuckles.

Bulges at the knuckles are a sure sign of a love of order, of a painstaking approach to whatever the person does. Pale, narrow nails are a sign of limited physical energy. These two factors would seem to indicate that this person does not act quickly or spontaneously. However, wide spaces between the fingers as the hand is positioned on a tabletop are a sign that the person is capable of much more spontaneous action than the other two configurations would demonstrate. For the most part, this person is very quick to respond to what is going on around him or her. The thorough and painstaking qualities would perhaps be reserved for special projects, and the limited energy shown by narrow nails is being utilized to full capacity.

AN APPROACH TO COMPATIBILITY

The aptitude for balancing traits found in the hands is crucial to the analysis of personal compatibility. Often, one partner can supply what is lacking in the other or can support tendencies already present. A sample of how this might work:

- Flat Mount of Venus.
- Sloping head line.
- Curving heart line.
- Fine skin texture.

A is a very emotional person who dreams of more than he or she can accomplish, given the low energy indicated by a flat Mount of Venus. The emotional and imaginative energies outstrip the physical energy. The emotional energy needs to be channeled, and a program of physical fitness undertaken. This will increase the physical vitality.

- Coarse skin texture.
- Curving heart line.
- Broad hand.

B is an emotional, warm, loving, demonstrative person who needs to be active. Unless another sign negates the trait, B possesses self-confidence. B needs to learn to be more attentive to sensitivities in others that are not native to B.

A and B are compatible emotionally, as shown by the curving heart lines. This is especially important since the curving heart line shows a need to act out what is felt.

A can teach B the value of working and resting in cycles and can provide ideas for the activity B desires. A's sloping head line shows a love of adventure. B's hand shows all the necessary energy for the creation of excitement and adventure. With patience, B can help A to act out A's dreams and to expand in activity and energy. Together, they can grow in adventure and expanded horizons.

Whether you are reading the hands of a couple or of an individual, the goal of analysis is to see and understand basic patterns, to note opposing traits, and to move to a synthesis capturing the essence of the whole personality.

21

Introduction to the Dictionary of Traits

Welcome to the fascinating world of human potential, as seen from the hands. Hands and their meaning have captured the imagination of people from the beginning of time. Famous prehistoric handprints are found in caves in France and other parts of the world. Ancient manuscripts attest that the study of hands dates back to the time of Aristotle.

Interest in hand reading persisted throughout changing civilizations in Egypt, Greece, and Rome. Although Gypsies did indeed carry forward the thread of this ancient divinatory art, the subject was also studied in universities in Europe during the sixteenth and early seventeenth centuries. Scientific investigations into the scope and usefulness of hand analysis began then and continue to this day.

Closer to our time, in the early twentieth century, an American, William G. Benham, published *The Laws of Scientific Hand Reading*. Benham was acquainted with all the ancient ways of interpreting hands. He tried them all, and in the process, added to his study many of the features we use today.

Reflecting the spirit of his time, Benham did much to put the art of palmistry on a scientific footing. He produced a groundbreaking work, *How to Choose Vocations From the Hand*, a book that helped people know, from the information in their hands, how best to fit into a newly industrialized society. What job was right? What career would bring fulfillment? His information, if it were updated to a twenty-first century outlook and geared to all the types of work available today, would be a welcome addition to the guidelines of any human resources department.

His portrayal of human potential seen in the hands is profound, and his system, along with other points of hand analysis, will be put to work in our Dictionary of Traits.

READER'S GUIDE TO THE DICTIONARY

This guide is designed especially for the first-time reader. You will need to know something about the ten points of analysis, and the meaning of the terms used to describe the hands' features.

In the dictionary, hands are analyzed according to these ten points: size, shape, length, color, consistency, texture, flexibility, mounts, lines, and gestures.

Feature:	Variations:	Applies to:
Size	Small, medium, large	Hands, mounts, nails
Shape	Round, square, spatulate, pointed	Palms, fingertips, nails
Length	Long, short	Palms, all fingers, each individual finger, finger sections (phalanges), fingernails
Color	Pink, pale, red, yellow, blue	Palms, nails
Consistency	Hard, firm, medium firm, soft, very soft	Palms, mounts
Texture	Fine, medium, coarse	Skin on back of hands
Flexibility	Easy movement, stiff movement	Fingers, thumbs

Feature:	Consists of:	Names:
Mounts	8 areas of the palm	Jupiter, Saturn, Apollo, Mercury, Venus, Luna, Upper Mars, Lower Mars
Lines	4 major lines	Life line, head line, heart line, fate line
	3 minor lines	Apollo line, Mercury line, line of intuition

Gestures   Movements of the
hands and fingers

To help you understand all the clues in the hands that are listed in the Dictionary, let's look at a capsule version of what these features mean.

Meaning of the Features

Size. Large hands—Show people who work well with details, are good planners and act on their ideas.

Small hands—Refer to people who "think big," the dreamers of the world.

Large mounts—Indicate a great deal of energy devoted to the areas of life the mount represents.

Small mounts—Show less energy dedicated to the areas of life the mount represents.

Large nails—An energetic person with mechanical ability, enjoys craft projects, building or fixing things.

Small nails—Less energetic person, quick to draw conclusions when forming new impressions.

Shape. Round palms, fingertips, or nails—Show a friendly, adaptable person.

Square palms, fingertips, or nails—Indicate a hardworking, result-oriented person.

Spatulate palms, fingertips, or nails—Belong to high-energy, innovative, restless people.

Pointed fingertips—Are not common, reveal an intuitive, psychic person who loves beauty, and enjoys living "in the now."

Length. Long palms—People who have long memories, are likely to be the family historian; meditative, creative personalities.

Short Palms—Persons who are quick to adapt to life's circumstances and events.

Long Fingers—Love of details; loyal personalities.

Short Fingers—Impatient; intuitive, impulsive personalities.

Long Fingernails—Love of beauty; peaceful, people-oriented personalities.

Short Fingernails—Keen, critical faculty; action-oriented personalities.

Note: the length of a nail in palmistry does not include the manicured part of a nail, just the area below the manicure.

Color. Pink—The most positive color for the palm and nails. Shows an optimistic, happy or contented nature, and a desire for activity, friendship, and love.

Pale—A pale tone to the palm or the nails indicates low energy, less interest in life and activity; a quiet or subdued personality, a person who feels burdened by circumstances.

Red—This color can be found on the whole palm, on just one or two areas of the palm, or on the nails. Means an excitable, high-energy person.

Yellow—Yellow tones on the palm show a cautious, sometimes cynical nature, a skeptic.

Blue—A blue color on the palms or the nails may signal a health problem or low energy, which should only be confirmed by a doctor. Diagnosing health should be reserved for health-care professionals.

Consistency. Soft hands—A kind person, one who is slow to make dreams or intentions a reality; strong emotional energy.

Very soft hands—Under-motivated or content to drift at times.

Medium firm hands—More motivated; a good level of energy to apply to daily tasks.

Firm hands—Very motivated; achievers who will reach their goals.

Hard hands—Stubborn; can apply pressure to make sure things go their way; strong physical energy.

Texture. Fine skin—Very sensitive, receptive. Seldom misses a thing, very observant; enjoys assimilating information.

Medium skin—Active, needs to be involved with people and projects to feel fulfilled.

Coarse skin—Not overly sensitive; needs outlets for a high level of energy; enjoys outdoor activities.

Flexibility. Flexibility is found in the fingers: where they join the palm, at the fingertips, and in the thumb.

Flexible fingers—Show a talented, outgoing person, quick to adapt to change; likes to move about in the world.

Stiff fingers—A more reserved nature; a cautious personality.

Flexible fingertips—A "quick study," someone who absorbs information effortlessly; a mimic; language ability.

Stiff fingertips—A cautious mindset, a reluctance to try something new, unless the benefit of the project can be surmised in advance.

Flexible thumbs—Indicate a spontaneous approach to life, an adaptable nature.

Stiff thumbs—A primary indication of someone who can "just say no," good boundaries and a resistance to peer pressure.

Mounts. Divisions—The palm is divided into eight separate areas, each with its own name and meaning.

Names—Originally, the names of Roman gods were used to describe the mounts and their meanings, and these traditional names still label the mounts. The mounts are called Jupiter, Saturn, Apollo, Mercury, Venus, Luna, Upper Mars, and Lower Mars.

Location on the hand—The Jupiter mount is located just below the index finger. The Saturn and Apollo mounts usually are combined into one mount located between the middle and ring fingers, while the Mercury mount is below the little finger. The Venus mount is formed by the ball of the thumb, and the Luna mount is across from the Venus mount, forming the outside edge of the palm. Upper Mars lies above the Luna mount, and Lower Mars sits at the top of the Venus mount, just inside the life line (p. 105).

Marks on the mounts—A variety of marks can be found on the mounts. In the dictionary, a selected number of them contribute to the definition of a trait (p. 114).

Vertical lines—These add strength to the mount's positive meaning.

Bar lines—These lines mean interference or obstacles to success in the area of life the mount represents.

Diagonal lines—These lines are a positive influence, showing the ability to network and make new contacts.

Triangles—A triangle is rarely found on mounts, but, if found, most often shows up on the Luna or Jupiter mounts. On any mount, a triangle indicates creativity, talent, and progress in the area of life related to the mount.

Grilles (also called Cross-hatch lines)—This pattern shows a bottled-up energy that may indicate disturbance, or challenges in the area of life connected to the mount.

Meanings of the Mounts: Here is a list of brief meanings for the mounts:

Jupiter—Refers to career, leadership ability, political ability, self-confidence.

Saturn—Signals a conservative nature, a concern for values, good judgment, common sense, a love of solitude, and an interest in science and research.

Apollo—Stands for resourcefulness, a creative personality with a cheerful, spontaneous nature; one who loves art and beauty.

Mercury—Indicates a quick and responsive mind; intuition and curiosity, ability for business, medicine, and psychology.

Venus—Focuses on home, family, and loved ones; abilities in music, dance, theater, self-expression; another indicator of love of beauty and harmony.

Luna—Shows a love of nature and scenery; a need to withdraw to contemplate personal experiences; an intuitive nature; attunement with the rhythms and cycles of life.

Mars—Upper Mars stands for strength, resistance to challenges, perseverance, courage, and high energy. Lower Mars indicates drive, physical strength, the ability to forge ahead in life.

Lines. Lines hold a complex amount of information. They define personality and potential, and predict many aspects of a person's life path. For this reason, lines must be analyzed according to their appearance and their variations.

Appearance. Long lines—Strong lines showing the potential for achievement and expansion in the areas of life they represent.

Short lines—Can signal a potential for restriction or challenges to growth in the areas of life related to the mount.

Deep lines—A sign of personal strength, motivation, and good health.

Shallow lines—Shallow or faintly drawn lines mean the traits they represent are not as ingrained in the personality and appear less often than traits indicated by a deep line.

Clear lines—Have no stray marks on them, are clearly drawn in the palm, and are easy to see. They indicate very positive use of their traits.

Fuzzy lines—These lines, which look a little fluffy, point to some hesitation about using their qualities and show periods of lowered motivation.

Straight lines—Express their potential more directly, demonstrating drive and ambition.

Curved lines—Show a flexible nature, a desire to speculate about the outcome of any action contemplated, a live-wire personality.

Wavy lines—Take flexibility to an extreme, can indicate vacillation or indecision, a tendency to get distracted.

Variations. Breaks—Interrupt the power of the line. A clean break is more dramatic, its effects more sudden. A break with overlapping ends tempers the significance of the break and means a more gradual period of change for the person (p. 115).

Chains—Weaken a line wherever they appear, adding indecision and confusion to the areas of life represented by the line (p. 115).

Islands—Restrict the energy of a line, signify obstacles or slower periods in the area of life experience related to the line (p. 115).

Falling branches—Small, fine lines drooping down from a major or minor line take away the power of the line to a certain extent; show possible disappointment or discouragement (p. 115).

Rising branches—Are very positive, boost the strength of a line; a sign of progress in life or increased good fortune (p. 113).

Forks—Lines may end in a two-prong or three-prong fork. Either version increases the scope of the line and adds to its meaning and potential (p. 115).

Marks on the Lines. Marks may appear on the lines, as well as on the mounts. A few of the lines' marks are:

Bar—Indicates interference or obstacles, some of which are internal challenges, such as discouragement, hesitation to act or believe in oneself (p. 114).

Cross—Also indicates interference and obstacles, often caused by outside events or conditions (p. 114).

Dots—Refer to tension or disruptions; sometimes refer to health matters (p. 114).

Square—Protects the line and its meaning, easing the way for efforts in the area of life related to the line (p. 114).

Gestures. Gestures, like the hands themselves, reveal much about a person, and a few examples will be found in the dictionary.

Fingers held wide apart—Sign of an independent personality, a free spirit who seeks adventure.

Fingers held close together—Show a cautious, conservative nature, people who want to be in control of their circumstances; good administrators.

Thumb held at a wide angle—A thumb held noticeably away from the palm signals an enterprising person; a powerful personality likely to make waves, to succeed in the world.

Thumb held close to the hand—A cautious nature, a tendency to be secretive or mum while pondering a future course of action.

Fingers curl in toward palm—A security-minded person, likes to double-check the facts before acting.

This is a great deal of information to process. Any way you can organize the material by category will help you to remember all that you have to consider. Here's an interesting fact:

Of the ten categories, only three require you to pick up and hold the hand you are examining: consistency, texture, and flexibility. You need to touch the palm to determine its consistency, and you have to touch the back of the hand to test its texture. You will need to stretch the fingers and thumb to get acquainted with their flexibility.

All the remaining categories—size, shape, length, color, mounts, lines and gestures—can be evaluated with or without touching the hand. If you make yourself aware of these seven categories while you analyze the first three, you'll find you can combine quite a bit of detail and arrive at conclusions from the moment you start your analysis.

KEY TO DICTIONARY TERMS

Many of the terms used to describe the hand are easily understood. A pink palm or a flexible thumb are uncomplicated clues, but because the lines and mounts contain a wide range of information, their descriptions are complex and more numerous.

The description of the lines on pages 180–181 gave you the key to their appearance and variations. There are two terms you will occasionally come across in the dictionary to describe a line:

Clear. This means the line is free of defects. The line has no dots, bars, or x's cutting across it and does not have islands, chains, or breaks.

Defective. If a line is described this way, the line has some or all of the above.

The mounts contain an amazing amount of information about personality, character, talent, energy, hopes, and dreams. Their appearance is analyzed by using three factors: height, firmness, and color.

To be developed, a mount must have:

Height. A mount must have some height, giving it the appearance of a small pad on the palm.

Firmness. A mount must be at least a little bit firm to indicate its qualities are being used.

Color. Pink is the color that activates a mount's meaning. Pink color on a mount is a bit like the red indicator light on your coffeemaker. When you see that light, you know your coffee is about to brew.

You notice that both a firm quality and a pink color mean that the mount's qualities are active. But here is a distinction that will let you know exactly what is going on with a person's energy:

A firm mount means that the mount's qualities have been developed and can be used at any time. A pink mount indicate that the mount's qualities are being used at the moment.

Combining these three factors of height, firmness, and color gives us a number of ways to describe a mount. When you encounter each term in the dictionary, you can refer to this chart if you want clarity about what exactly the description means. Each distinction is a key to correctly understanding the clue the mount offers.

+ (plus)	**This mount has:**
Developed	Some height, or firmness, or color.
Very developed	All three features are present, and one or more will be there in an outstanding amount—great height, or firmness, or much color.
Strongly developed	All three features are present, and two or more are present in outstanding amounts.
Highly developed	A lot of height, a firm or hard consistency, with a deep pink or red color.
Well-developed	All three features are present and balanced. The mount's height, firmness and color are evenly developed.
High	A pad that stands up noticeably in the palm.
Firm	A consistency that resists pressure when touched. The skin bounces back from momentary indentation when the mount is pressed.
Large	A wide area in the palm, taking up all the space designated for its placement.
Full	A wide area like a large mount, plus good height.
Well-formed	Height, firmness, and color are all in proportion. The mount is neither too tall or too hard, is pink rather than red.
Overly developed	All the features to excess: extremely high, hard and red in color.

Not every mount is developed—that is, showing good use of its qualities. Mounts can be under-developed when their qualities are dormant or nonexistent. Such mounts are described as follows.

- (minus)	**The Mount has:**
Not developed	A flat appearance in its assigned area. The mount does not make a little pad on the palm. The mount will not be pink in color.
Under-developed	Occasionally a mount will not only be flat, but appear to sag a bit. In this case, the consistency is very soft.
Flat	No cushion at all is detected in its assigned area. Area feels hard to the touch and close to the bone underneath.
Baggy	The area has a cushion, but the consistency is so soft, the mount appears to have little folds in it.

HOW TO USE THE DICTIONARY

At last, you are ready to use the dictionary. Most of us would like to know a little about ourselves and others from the hands, and in a few words. Now you can do that. The information has been pared down to the essentials, and the essential clues themselves have been listed in order of importance.

Here is the way to use the dictionary:

Bold Print. When you see a line in bold print, this is your signal that without this feature in the hand, you do not have the indicated trait. Bold print means that feature is absolutely essential to the personality trait being described.

Listing Order. After the initial entries in bold print, the clues are listed in descending order of importance. In many cases, the last clue listed is a general clue that could pertain to other features as well.

Value to Reader. As you apply the entries to a hand, you are at the same time learning what is and what is not important for each trait. In other words, as you use the dictionary, you have an opportunity to weigh and evaluate the role of every clue the hand has to offer. In some cases, a round shape is the first most important clue. In a later entry, round shape may appear last in the list. Knowing the order of the hand's clues will make you a quick and expert hand analyst.

Note. When you use the dictionary, you will find that some of the lines of description end in the word "with." This is a signal that that line's information must be taken together with the line that follows. Features described in both lines are necessary to indicate the trait. Occasionally you will find two lines in a row end in "with." Both of those lines plus the line following the second "with" are one unit. The features listed in all three lines are necessary to demonstrate the presence of the trait. When a line of description does not end in the word "with," that line stands alone as a clue to the trait.

ENJOY USING THE DICTIONARY

Now you have learned that hands, even in a short analysis, have as many as ten points to consider. There is more to analyze than just the lines on the palm. The whole hand provides clues to a person's potential. Because you have so much to consider, you may wonder where to begin.

The dictionary gets you off to a good start. You can see, in just a few features of the hands, a wide range of personality traits. You are able to start to analyze hands, whether you have read the entire book or whether you have read only this introductory guide to the dictionary.

If you know nothing of palmistry, you can learn in short order by using the dictionary. It will teach you how to observe a few clues in the hands and discover amazingly accurate details about the people in your life.

If you are an experienced palmist, with the dictionary you can test and succinctly apply what you already know.

People interested in hands are often also students of human nature. What better way to get to know something about a person than from their hands? You can observe hands openly or quietly. You can work interactively with clients, using all that you have learned. Or you can concentrate on a few clues and use them to observe a stranger's hands, say, while you are standing in a grocery store line.

For a moment you may think, "Analyze the hands of someone I'm not even talking to?" Of course! The beauty of palmistry is you can use what you know anywhere. Think how much fun you'll have getting to know a bit about your favorite media personalities every time you see their hands on television or in print on an almost daily basis. Getting to know people better—that's what palmistry is all about.

Enjoy your journey into the world of hands!

DICTIONARY

Active

Consistency: Firm hands
Mounts: Large Venus mount
Shape: Spatulate fingertips
Color: Pink color on palms, lines and
nails
Gestures: Fingers held wide apart

Adventurous

**Shape: Bottom of palm spatulate-
shaped**
Mounts: Venus and Luna mounts, both
large, well-developed
Flexibility: Very flexible fingers
Line Pattern: Life line runs diagonally
across the hand

Affectionate

Line Pattern: Long, curved heart line
Color: Pink heart line
Color: Pink color across the whole palm
Consistency: Soft or medium-soft palms
Mounts: All the upper mounts well-
developed

Aggressive

Consistency: Hard hand, with
Mounts: A prominent Lower Mars
    mount
Color: Palm surface and lines very red
Size: Thick thumb and thick palm
Shape: Spatulate palm, nails, and
fingertips

Agreeable

Shape: Round-shaped palms, fingers
    and nails
Line Pattern: Curved heart line, with
Color: Pink palm
Mounts: Upper mounts high and firm
Length: Index finger short-to-average
length

Alert

Mounts: High Mercury mount
Fingers: Long little finger
Texture: Smooth, fine skin
Mounts: Upper mounts developed
Line Pattern: Many lines on the palm

Ambitious

Fingers: Long index finger
Mounts: A well-developed Jupiter mount
Length: A long thumb
Size: Thick hands

Anxious

Line Pattern: Many fine lines crossing the palm
Size: Thin palm
Line Pattern: Major lines chained
Line Pattern: Bar lines on the heart line
Color: Pale or yellow color on palm

Argumentative

Mounts: Highly developed Lower Mars mount, with
Color: Red on Lower Mars mount, with
Line Pattern: Cross-hatch lines on Lower Mars mount
Color: Red lines
Mounts: Both Mars and Mercury mounts highly developed
Consistency: Hard hands

Assured (self-assured)

Length: Long index finger, long thumb
Consistency: Very firm palm
Length: Long ring finger
Mounts: Well-developed Upper Mars mount

Balanced

Length: Finger length evenly proportioned
Mounts: Evenly developed mounts (one not greatly larger or smaller)

Color: Even color across the palm (no red or white splotches)
Line Pattern: Absence of bar lines, breaks, chains, or islands on the major lines

Bold

Shape: Spatulate palm, nails, and fingertips
Size: Very fleshy palms, with
Mounts: A large Venus mount
Line Pattern: Head line widely separated from life line

Brave

Mounts: Upper Mars mount large and curved
Consistency: Firm palm

Broad-minded

Line Pattern: Wide space between head and heart lines
Line Pattern: Straight head line, ending under the ring finger

Business Ability

Line Pattern: A strong, well-defined Mercury line
Length: A long or medium-long little finger
Fingers: A strong, well-shaped middle finger
Shape: Spatulate fingernails, fingertips and palms
Fingers: A long thumb, with
Gesture: Thumb held at a wide angle away from the hand
Consistency: A firm palm

Calm

Mounts: A full Luna mount, with
Shape: A round shape to Luna
Thumb: A strong, well-formed thumb
Line Pattern: A deep, clear life line
Consistency: Firm palms

Caring

Consistency: Soft hands, with
Color: Pink hands
Line Pattern: A long heart line
Mounts: A well-developed Venus mount

Cautious

Line Pattern: Head line begins tied to
life line
Size: Thin palm, thin fingers
Line Pattern: Straight heart line, with
Mounts: A flat Venus mount
Color: Pale or yellow color on the palm

Changeable

Line Pattern: Wavy heart line and
wavy head line
Line Pattern: Long head line, line uneven, alternating between shallow and
deep
Length: Short thumb, short middle finger

Charming

Mounts: Venus and Luna mounts both
well-developed
Mounts: All mounts well-developed
Shape: Round palm, round fingertips
Color: Pink on palm

Competitive

Mounts: Both Upper and Lower Mars
well-developed
Consistency: Firm hands
Line Pattern: Head line widely separated
from life line
Shape: Spatulate nails, with
Gestures: Fingers held wide apart

Complex Personality

Line Pattern: Many fine lines on palm
Line Pattern: Long head line or a forked
head line
Length: Long palms, with
Size: Thin palm
Size: Difference in size of two hands
Length: Head and/or heart line different
length on right and left hands

Confident

Length: Long index finger
Mounts: Well-developed Jupiter mount
Line Pattern: Head line separated from
life line
Consistency: Firm palm

Conscientious

Shape: Square-shaped palms, finger-
tips, and nails
Length: Long middle finger
Length: Index and ring fingers equal in
length

Conservative

Line Pattern: Head line tied to life line at its beginning
Gestures: Fingers held close together
Shape: Square-shaped fingertips and nails
Consistency: Palms hard or very firm

Considerate

Consistency: Soft or medium-soft palm, with
Mounts: Well-developed upper mounts
Color: Pink color on palm, with
Consistency: Firm Venus mount

Controlled

Length: Long thumbs
Flexibility: Stiff thumbs
Shape: Square shape on palm, fingertips, nails
Line Pattern: Straight head line

Cordial

Color: Pink palms
Shape: Round-shaped palms, fingertips, and nails
Mounts: Upper mounts well-developed

Courageous

Mounts: Both Upper and Lower Mars mounts well-developed
Line Pattern: Long, deep Mercury line
Shape: Spatulate-shaped hands
Line Pattern: Straight, deep head line

Crabby (irritable)

Mounts: Prominent Lower Mars mount, with
Line Pattern: Stray or cross-hatched lines on Lower Mars mount
Line Pattern: Head and/or heart lines wavy, not straight
Line Pattern: Narrow quadrangle (space between head and heart lines)

Creative

Line Pattern: Head line long and curved down into Luna mount
Mounts: Well-developed Apollo mount
Fingers: A long ring finger
Line Pattern: A series of vertical lines on the bottom half of Venus mount
Shape: Spatulate-shaped ring finger

Critical

Mounts: Flat Luna mount, with
Color: Pale hands
Mounts: Large Mercury mount, with
Line Pattern: Mercury mount covered with fine lines
Mounts: Large Lower Mars mount, with
Finger: A short little finger

Curious

Shape: Top of palm and fingertips spatulate-shaped
Line Pattern: Long head line
Mounts: High Mercury mount, well-developed Saturn mount
Line Pattern: Forked head line
Shape: Round palm, with
Color: Pink on palm

Decisive

Length: Long thumb tip
Size: Thick thumb
Flexibility: Stiff thumb, straight, with no curve between tip and next section
Head line: Straight head line
Shape: Square-shaped palm and fingertips

Defensive

Line Pattern: Head line starts inside life line
Line Pattern: Numerous fine cross-hatch lines in center of palm
Color: Very pale palm

Deliberate

Length: Long fingers
Shape: Square palm, fingertips, and nails
Length: Long palm
Size: Thin palm, thin fingers
Length: Long middle finger

Demanding

Size: Thick palm and fingers
Consistency: Hard palms
Size: Thick, fleshy thumb
Flexibility: Inflexible thumb

Dependable

Line Pattern: Head line even in depth, free of breaks or stress marks
Length: Long thumb
Shape: Thumb contoured, with thin second section
Shape: Square-shaped palms and finger-tips

Devoted

Line Pattern: Long, curved heart line
Line Pattern: Heart line ends under index finger
Mounts: Strong, well-formed Venus mount
Line Pattern: Forked heart line
Color: Pink color on palm and lines

Diplomatic

Fingers: "Waisted" thumb (middle section has thin, sculpted shape)
Shape: Pointed thumb tip
Length: Long little finger
Shape: Round or pointed fingertips

Direct

Length: Short fingers
Length: Short little finger, in particular
Size: Thick second section on thumb
Gestures: Wide spaces between fingers

Disciplined

Length: Long thumb, with
Consistency: Firm hands
Line Pattern: Straight head line
Shape: Square-shaped hands
Finger Pattern: Long, deep fate line

Distracted

Line Pattern: Head line wavy or broken
Line Pattern: Numerous fine lines on palm
Flexibility: Very flexible thumb
Consistency: Soft hands

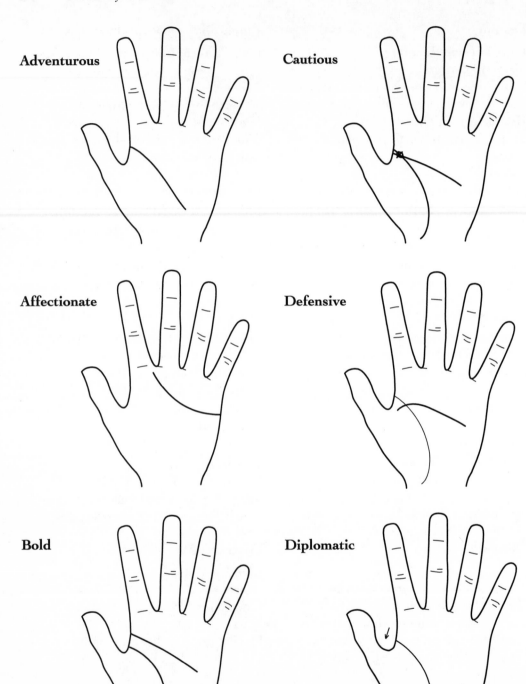

Adventurous

Cautious

Affectionate

Defensive

Bold

Diplomatic

Eager

Length: Short fingers
Shape: Spatulate fingertips and nails
Gestures: Wide space between fingers

Economical

Flexibility: Stiff thumb, tip does not bend
Size: Thin fingers
Shape: Fingers very thin at bottom sections, where fingers meet palm
Shape: Square-shaped palm and fingertips

Eloquent

Mounts: Well-developed Mercury mount
Length: Long tip on little finger
Mounts: Strong, firm Jupiter mount
Length: Long index finger

Emotional

Line Pattern: Curved heart line, heart line widely forked
Mounts: Full Venus mount
Line Pattern: Heart line deeply etched in hand
Line Pattern: Heart line has numerous branches under little finger
Line Pattern: Wavy heart line

Empathic

Mounts: Jupiter, Saturn, Apollo, and Mercury mounts highly developed
Mounts: Luna mount high and firm
Color: Pink color on palm, especially on Luna mount

Line Pattern: Diagonal lines on Luna mount

Energetic

Consistency: Firm palm, with
Color: Pink palm
Mounts: Well-developed, highly padded mounts
Size: Wide nails

Enterprising

Consistency: Firm palm
Size: Wide palm
Shape: Spatulate shapes on palm, fingertips, and nails

Enthusiastic

Shape: Spatulate- or round-shaped palms and fingers
Color: Pink on palm, with
Mounts: A high Venus mount
Mounts: Well-developed Lower Mars mount
Line Pattern: Forked heart line

ESP Ability

Mounts: All mounts high and well-developed, especially Luna and Mercury
Shape: Pointed fingertips
Line Pattern: An "x" in the space between the head and heart lines

Excitable

Mounts: High Mercury mount, with
Length: Short fingers overall
Length: Short little finger
Flexibility: Very flexible fingers
Line Pattern: Numerous fine lines on the palm
Size: Narrow nails

Extroverted

Line Pattern: Wide arc to life line
Shape: Round shape to base of nails, nail surface dome-shaped
Line Pattern: Head line widely separated from life line
Line Pattern: Lines deeply etched in hands
Color: Pink color on palm

Fair

Line Pattern: Wide, even space between the head and heart lines
Size: Both hands same size
Length: Fingers of average length, no finger very long or too short
Color: Both lines and palm have a good color, not pale, yellow- or blue-toned
Gestures: Thumb held straight and close to the palm

Fatigued

Color: Pale colored palms
Line Pattern: Light lines, faintly etched in palms
Consistency: Very soft hands
Mounts: Two or more mounts "baggy," resembling deflated balloons

Fearful

Mounts: Upper Mars mount flat
Shape: Center of palm "hollow," with tendons raised up, dips between them
Color: Pale hands
Size: Thin hands

Feeling-oriented

Mounts: Well-developed mounts
Shape: Round palm and fingertips
Line Pattern: Long heart line
Line Pattern: Forked heart line

Forgetful

Line Pattern: Head line short or broken, fuzzy or lightly etched on the palm
Line Pattern: Island on the head line
Color: Blue-tinged color on Venus mount
Color: Purple color near moons at base of nails

Free Thinker

Line Pattern: Wide space between the head and life lines
Flexibility: Fingers very flexible at their base, where they join the palm
Gestures: Wide spaces between the fingers

Friendly

Shape: Round shape to palm, fingertips, and nails
Line Pattern: Curved heart line
Mounts: High Venus mount
Consistency: Soft hands
Color: Pink color on palms and lines

Line Pattern: Diagonal slant or wide arc
to life line
Mounts: All upper mounts well-
developed

Frustrated

**Consistency: Lower Mars mount is
soft, with**
**Line Pattern: A grille (cross-hatched
lines) on Lower Mars mount**
Line Pattern: Cross-hatched lines on
palm, particularly cutting through life
line
Line Pattern: Horizontal bar lines on
fingertips
Color: Pale palms
Consistency: Soft hands
Mounts: Upper Mars mount flat

Fulfilled

**Line Pattern: Major lines clear, deep,
and without breaks, islands, or bar
lines**
Consistency: Good skin tone, consistency
neither too soft nor too hard
Line Pattern: Well-developed fate line

Fun-loving

**Mounts: Large Venus mount and a
well-developed Apollo mount**
Length: Long ring finger
Line Pattern: Major lines clear, no
crosses or stray marks on them
Line Pattern: Life line with a wide arc,
slanting diagonally to Luna mount

Generous

**Flexibility: Thumb tip bends backward
when thumb is extended**
**Line Pattern: Heart line long and
curved, or forked at the end**
Line Pattern: Wide space between head
and heart lines
Color: Pink color on palm
Mounts: Full Venus and Luna mounts

Go-getter

Shape: Spatulate-shaped fingertips
Size: Wide palm
Consistency: Firm palm
Length: Long index finger
Mounts: All mounts well-developed

Gracious

Length: Long fingers, with
Mounts: Round, full Venus mount
Shape: Oval or round base to fingernails
Color: Pink palm
Mounts: All mounts developed

Grounded (practical)

Line Pattern: Deep lines
Line Pattern: Straight head line
Shape: Square-shaped palms
Mounts: Well-developed Saturn mount
Line Pattern: No stray marks crossing
the major lines
Line Pattern: Even space between head
and heart lines

Happy
Shape: Round shape predominant in hand—palms, fingertips, nails
Line Pattern: Clear, curved heart line
Mounts: Apollo mount well-developed
Color: Pink color on the palm
Line Pattern: Head line average length

Hasty
Shape: Spatulate-shaped palm, fingertips, and nails
Length: Short fingers
Length: Short little finger, in particular
Gestures: Wide spaces between fingers

Healthy
Line Pattern: Major lines deep, free from islands, chains, and breaks
Line Pattern: Major lines also free from bar lines and dots
Consistency: Firm palm
Color: Light pink color on palm and nails
Special Feature: Nails are without vertical or horizontal ridges
Color: Nails are not tinged with white, blue, or purple tones

Helpful
Mounts: All mounts well-developed, especially Venus and Jupiter mounts
Line Pattern: Fate line starting on Luna mount
Length: Straight, long index finger

Hermit
Lines: Head line begins inside life line or tied to life line at beginning
Size: Thin to medium-thin palms and fingers

Lines: Narrow arc to life line
Mounts: Small or flat mount of Venus
Color: Pale color on palm
Mounts: Luna mount overly developed

Hospitable
Consistency: Soft palms
Color: Pink palms
Mounts: Large Jupiter and Apollo mounts
Line Pattern: Forked heart line
Fingers: Thumb tip curves backward

Humorous (sense of humor)
Mounts: Mercury mount well-developed
Special Feature: Skin ridge loop on palm below ring and little fingers
Special Feature: One or more whorl-pattern fingerprints

Hypersensitive
Size: Very thin hands, with
Shape: Hollow palm (dip in center of palm, making tendons visible)
Color: Heightened red color on palm and nails
Color: Blue color on Venus mount
Line Pattern: Faint lines, broken lines, stray cross-hatch marks on palm

Idealistic
Shape: Pointed fingertips
Size: Thin palm
Size: Thin fingers
Length: Long fingers
Line Pattern: Straight heart line

Empathic

Fair

ESP Ability

Frustrated

Extroverted

Hermit

Impatient

Length: Short fingers
Size: Wide, thick palm
Mounts: Strongly developed Lower Mars
mount
Color: Red coloring on palms

Impractical

Shape: Pointed fingertips
Size: Slender hand
Line Pattern: Head line dipping into
Luna mount
Flexibility: Fingers and thumb extremely
flexible
Length: Short middle finger

Impressionable

Line Pattern: Wavy head line
Mounts: Large Mercury mount, with
cross-hatch lines on it
Size: Long, narrow nails

Inconsistent

Line Pattern: Wavy head line and heart
line
Line Pattern: Absent or faintly etched
fate line
Line Pattern: Many small stray lines
crossing the palm

Indecisive

Length: Second section of thumb very
long
Special Feature: Composite (double
loop) fingerprint on thumb or middle
finger
Line Pattern: Wavy head line

Independent

Line Pattern: Head line begins
separated from life line
Shape: Spatulate shape to palms, nails,
or fingertips
Gestures: Wide spaces between the
fingers
Size: Thick palms, with
Shape: Square palms
Line Pattern: Very straight head line

Influential

Mounts: Prominent Jupiter mount
Length: Long index finger
Length: Long thumb
Mounts: All mounts well-developed
Length: Long thumb tip

Inhibited

Line Pattern: Narrow arc to life line
Color: Pale color on palm

Innovative

Shape: Any spatulate shape in the
hand: nails, palms, or fingertips
Mounts: Highly developed Mercury and
Apollo mounts
Length: Long middle sections in finger
phalanges

Insecure

Line Pattern: Many fine lines scattered
along palm in a random pattern
Fingers: Little finger bends inward toward palm
Gestures: Little finger pulled back, out of
line with rest of fingers
Length: Very short little finger

Flexibility: Fingers stiff, with
Gestures: Fingers held close together

Insightful

Mounts: Large Mercury and Luna mounts
Mounts: All upper mounts well-developed
Line Pattern: Line of intuition (crescent-shaped line near outside edge of palm)
Line Pattern: Strong Mercury line

Jittery

Line Pattern: Several bar lines crossing the heart line
Line Pattern: Bar (horizontal) lines on fingertips
Mounts: Lower Mars mount has a grille, or bar lines, with
Line Pattern: Life line slants in a wide diagonal arc

Joyful

Color: Pink color on palms and lines
Mounts: Large Venus and Apollo mounts
Line Pattern: Forked heart line, especially if with three prongs (trident)

Judgmental

Consistency: Hard palm, with
Shape: Square-shaped palms
Consistency: Soft palm, with
Color: Yellow tone on palm
Color: Pale tone on palm
Line Pattern: Many fine lines on palm, with
Flexibility: Stiff fingers

Kind

Consistency: Soft hands, with
Color: Pink color on palm, lines, and nails
Line Pattern: Long, curved heart line
Mounts: Venus mount full, soft
Line Pattern: Vertical lines across the bottom of Venus mount

Knowledgeable

Line Pattern: Long, slightly curved head line
Mounts: All mounts highly developed
Mounts: Mercury mount strongly developed

Lazy

Consistency: Soft hands, with
Color: Pale color
Line Pattern: Fate line absent
Line Pattern: Lines faintly etched in hands, with
Consistency: Soft mounts
Line Pattern: Main lines have a fuzzy appearance

Leader

Length: Long index finger, long well-shaped thumb
Line Pattern: Head line begins on the Jupiter mount
Mounts: Large Jupiter mount
Line Pattern: Head line begins widely separated from life line

Humorous

Insightful

Humorous

Knowledgeable

Indecisive

Leader

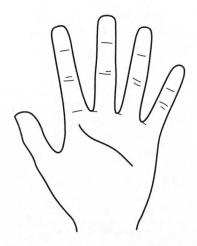

Loving

Line Pattern: Curved heart line
Consistency: Soft hands
Mounts: Well-developed Venus mount
Color: Pink color on palm

Loyal

Length: Long fingers
Shape: Square palm, square fingertips
and nails

Lucky

**Mount: Mercury and Apollo mounts
well-developed**
**Line Pattern: A few small vertical lines
on Mercury mount**
Line Pattern: Long vertical line between
two smaller parallel lines on Apollo
Length: Long ring finger
Special Feature: Fingers set squarely on
palm, wide spaces between fingers

Managerial Ability

**Length: Long index finger and long
thumb**
Mounts: Large Jupiter mount
Line Pattern: Head line begins separated
from life line

Marketing Ability

**Line Pattern: Head line begins widely
separated from life line**
Line Pattern: Fate line starts on Luna
mount
Line Pattern: Wide space between head
and heart lines
Line Pattern: Wide arc to life line

Line Pattern: Diagonal lines on Luna
mount

Mechanical Ability

**Mounts: Well-developed Mars and Sat-
urn mounts**
Line Pattern: Straight head line
Shape: Square- or spatulate-shaped
fingertips

Meditative

**Length: Long Saturn finger, long tip on
Saturn finger**
Fingers: Ring finger leans toward middle
finger
Length: Long palms
Size: Thin hands

Melancholy

Length: Very long middle finger, with
**Mounts: Highly developed Saturn
mount**
Color: Pale or yellow color on palm
Mounts: All mounts flat
Length: Long palm
Size: Thin palm

Methodical

Shape: Square-shaped hands and nails
Shape: Square fingertips, with
Line Pattern: A very straight head line

Mistrusting

Consistency: Hard palm, with
**Color: Yellow or pale white tone on
palm**
Length: Long middle finger
Mounts: Saturn mount highly developed

Motivated

Mounts: Lower Mars mount highly developed and firm, with
Color: Pink or red color on Lower Mars mount
Consistency: Firm palm
Length: Long thumb

Nature-loving

Mounts: Large Luna mount, highly developed Jupiter mount
Mounts: Well-developed Saturn mount, with
Length: Long middle section on middle finger
Length: Long base sections on all the fingers (section nearest palm)

Neat

Shape: Square-shaped palms, nails, and fingertips
Line Pattern: Straight head line on both palms

Neglectful

Line Pattern: Head line wavy, broken, or with an island on it
Line Pattern: Head line faintly etched in hand, while other lines are deep
Line Pattern: Fuzzy appearance to head line
Mounts: Large Lower Mars mount with a flat Upper Mars mount

Negotiating Ability

Fingers: Long, straight little finger, with
Mounts: A well-developed Mercury mount
Consistency: A very firm palm
Length: Long thumb
Flexibility: Thumb rigid, resisting pressure when touched

Nervous

Size: Thin hands, with
Line Pattern: Fine lines traced all across the palm
Line Pattern: Broken Mercury line
Line Pattern: Series of bar lines on heart line

Nonconformist

Shape: Spatulate-shaped palms and nails
Shape: Spatulate fingertips
Color: Heightened pink or red color on palm
Gestures: Fingers held wide apart

Nurturing

Line Pattern: Long and clear, curved, forked, and deeply traced heart line
Color: Pink color on palm
Mounts: Mount of Venus high and firm, with
Line Pattern: Vertical lines on Venus mount

Objective

Line Pattern: Wide space between heart and head lines
Line Pattern: Very straight head line
Shape: Square shape fingertips

Obliging

Consistency: Soft palms
Flexibility: Fingers very flexible
Color: Pink color on palm
Flexibility: Flexible thumb, offers no resistance when touched
Length: Short thumb

Observant

Mounts: Mercury mount high
Mounts: All upper mounts well-developed
Length: Long little finger
Mounts: Luna mount highly developed

Obstinate

Size: Thick, heavy thumb
Consistency: Hard palm, with
Length: Short, straight head line
Size: Thick hands, with
Consistency: Medium or hard palms
Length: Thumb tip very long

Old-fashioned

Shape: Very square shape to hands, with
Length: Long palms
Line Pattern: Deep, short head line
Special Feature: Outside edge of hand very flat

Open-minded

Line Pattern: Wide space between head and heart line
Line Pattern: Head line begins widely separated from life line
Line Pattern: Long heart line, ending in a triple-prong fork
Line Pattern: Fate line begins on Luna mount

Opinionated

Length: Long thumb, with
Flexibility: Stiff thumb
Gestures: Thumb held close to hand
Flexibility: Stiff hands, with
Size: Thick fingertips
Line Pattern: Long, straight, very deep head line

Optimistic

Line Pattern: Heart line curved and clear, with no stray marks on it
Color: Pink color on palm
Line Pattern: No stray lines cutting through the life line

Orderly

Shape: Square palm, nails, and fingertips
Line Pattern: Head line clear with no bar lines, islands, or breaks

Organized

Length: Long, strong thumb
Consistency: Firm palm
Shape: Square palm, nails, and fingertips
Line Pattern: Head line clear with no bar lines, islands, or breaks

Overbearing

Size: Thick hands, thick thumb
Consistency: Hard or very hard palms
Flexibility: Stiff hands

Overcautious

Shape: Square palms and square middle fingertip
Length: Long middle finger
Length: Long fingers
Size: Thin hands

Overconfident

Flexibility: Very flexible fingers, with
Gestures: Fingers held wide apart
Line Pattern: Head line begins separated from life line
Mounts: A very developed Jupiter mount

Patient

Length: Long fingers
Color: Absence of very deep pink or red color on palm
Mounts: Well-developed Upper Mars mount
Mounts: Large Luna mount
Gestures: Fingers held close together

Peacemaker

Line Pattern: Curved head line, ending in a double- or triple-prong fork
Color: Pink color on palm
Shape: Round fingertips and nails
Line Pattern: Slightly curved head line

People-oriented

Shape: Round fingernails, with
Line Pattern: Curved heart line
Line Pattern: Wide arc to life line
Mounts: Full, firm Venus mount

Perceptive

Mounts: Large, well-developed Luna mount
Mounts: All upper mounts well-developed
Line Pattern: An "x" in the space between the head and heart lines
Line Pattern: Diagonal (slanting) lines on Luna mount
Line Pattern: A triangle on Luna mount

Perfectionist

Shape: Square-shaped nails and fingertips
Shape: Bottom of palm square shaped
Shape: Outside edge of hand (percussion) flat and straight
Special Feature: Skin ridge loop between the middle and ring fingers

Persevering

Mounts: Upper Mars mount well-developed, with
Consistency: Firm hands
Length: Long thumb or a very long thumb tip
Shape: Broad thumb

Personable

Mount: Large Venus mount, with
Line Pattern: Vertical lines at base of
  Venus mount
Shape: Round palms, fingertips, and nails
Fingers: Well-formed thumb with "waist-
  ed" second phalange
Length: Average to long ring finger
Line Pattern: Fate line starts on Luna
  mount

Persuasive

Fingers: Little fingertip curves toward
  ring finger
Length: Very long little finger
Shape: Little finger has a pointed tip
Length: Long thumb, with
Mounts: Large Lower Mars mount

Pessimistic

Size: Thin hands, with
Length: Long middle finger
Color: Yellow tone on palm
Mounts: Large Saturn mount
Line Pattern: Head line end curves
  downward, ends on Luna mount

Pioneering

Shape: Spatulate-shaped palm, finger-
  tips, and nails
Consistency: Firm palm
Size: Wide nails
Color: Pink tone on palm
Mounts: Upper mounts well-developed

Plainspoken

Size: Thick second section on thumb
Length: Short little finger

Pleasant

Shape: Oval shaped nails, round palms,
  with
Color: Pink color in nails and palm
Mounts: All mounts well-developed
Line Pattern: Few or no stress lines

Poised

Length: Long little finger
Fingers: All fingers straight and well-
  shaped
Length: Long middle finger
Mounts: Well-developed Venus mount

Political Ability

Mount: large Jupiter mount, with
Line Pattern: Head line starts on
  Jupiter mount
Gestures: Thumb held away from hand,
  jutting up at a noticeable angle
Size: Thick hands
Shape: Spatulate base to palm

Positive

Line Pattern: Curved heart line, with
Color: Pink color on palm and lines
Fingers: All held straight, no bends or
  curves
Mounts: A firm Jupiter mount

Lucky

Personable

Perceptive

Persuasive

Perfectionist

Plainspoken

Possessive

Line Pattern: Heart line ends high on palm, between index and middle fingers
Shape: Dome-shaped nails
Flexibility: Stiff fingers

Powerful

Size: Big hands, thick hands, thick fingers
Length: Long thumb
Mounts: All mounts highly developed
Consistency: Firm palm

Practical

Line Pattern: Straight head line
Shape: Square-shaped palm
Length: Fingers medium-long

Precise

Shape: Square-shaped palms and nails
Line Pattern: Short, straight head line

Productive

Mounts: Large Upper and Lower Mars mounts
Length: Long thumb
Flexibility: Moderately flexible thumb
Shape: Square-shaped hands, nails, and fingertips
Length: Long index finger
Line Pattern: Long fate line running the length of the palm

Progressive

Shape: Spatulate-shaped hands, nail, and fingertips
Line Pattern: Head line starts separated from life line

Proud

Length: Long index finger
Mounts: High Jupiter and Saturn mounts
Flexibility: Stiff fingers

Prudent

Mounts: Well-developed Saturn mount
Length: Long Saturn finger
Mounts: Remaining mounts evenly developed, not too flat or too high
Line Pattern: Straight head line
Shape: Square shape to hand and nails

Psychic

Shape: Pointed fingertips
Line Pattern: Intuition line on Luna mount
Line Pattern: A small cross between head and heart lines (Mystic cross)
Line Pattern: Head line begins under Saturn mount
Mounts: All upper mounts well-developed
Special Feature: A triangle on Luna mount

Purposeful

Consistency: Firm hands
Length: Long thumbs
Line Pattern: Straight or very slightly curved head line

Pushover

Flexibility: Thumb very flexible, offers no resistance to touch
Length: Very short thumb
Size: Thin hands
Consistency: Very soft hands
Shape: Flat palms, mounts not developed
Mounts: Mercury and Venus mounts overdeveloped
Line Pattern: Head line ending deep in Luna mount

Pushy

Size: Large thumb, with
Shape: Fleshy, poorly shaped thumb
Size: Thick, fleshy hands, with
Color: Bright pink or red color on palm
Consistency: Hard hands

Quality-conscious

Mounts: Strong Saturn mount
Shape: Square hands
Line Pattern: Straight head line
Shape: Base of palm and bottom of second thumb joint sharply squared

Quarrelsome

Color: Red color on whole palm surface, with
Consistency: Hard hands, with
Mounts: Very large Mars mounts
Consistency: Very soft hands, with

Color: Very pale hands
Line Pattern: Numerous fine lines crossing the palm in a random pattern

Questioning

Length: Long middle fingers
Mounts: Strong Saturn mount
Shape: Spatulate nails
Mounts: Well-developed Mercury mount

Quiet

Gesture: Thumb held close to palm, all fingers held close together
Size: Thin palm
Shape: Flat palm
Color: Pale skin tone

Quitter

Mounts: Flat Upper Mars mount
Size: Small thumb
Length: Short thumb
Consistency: Very soft palm, with
Line Pattern: Stray lines across the palm
Mounts: Flat Venus mount

Realistic

Line Pattern: Straight head line
Line Patterns: Head, heart, and life lines all deep and clear
Shape: Square shape to palm, fingertips and nails
Special Feature: All features evenly developed: size, length, and mounts

Reasonable

Special Feature: All features balanced
Line Pattern: Wide space between head and heart lines

Line Pattern: Head line slightly curved, higher in hand, not ending on Luna

Rebellious

Line Pattern: Head line begins very widely separated from life line
Gestures: Thumb held at a wide angle, away from hand
Mounts: Highly developed Lower Mars mount, with
Line Pattern: Numerous lines on Lower Mars mount
Line Pattern: Head line starting inside life line on Lower Mars mount
Line Pattern: Head line broken, with ends overlapping (not a clean break)

Receptive

Consistency: Soft hands
Shape: Round palms, nails, and fingertips
Line Pattern: Curved heart line
Line Pattern: Heart line ends high on Jupiter mount

Reckless

Line Pattern: Head line begins widely separated from life line
Shape: Spatulate palm
Length: Short thumb
Length: Short middle finger

Reclusive

Length: Long palms, with
Size: Thin palms
Mounts: Highly developed Saturn mount

Length: Long middle finger
Color: Pale color on palm
Line Pattern: Narrow space between head and heart lines (the quadrangle)

Reformer

Size: Thick palms and fingers
Shape: Spatulate palm, nails, and fingertips
Length: Long index finger, long little finger
Mounts: Strong Mars mounts
Line Pattern: Straight, deep head line

Reliable

Shape: Square shape palms, nails, and fingertips, with
Line Pattern: Straight head line
Mounts: All mounts evenly developed
Mounts: Upper Mars mount highly developed

Remote

Size: Thin fingers, thin and narrow palm
Mounts: Luna mount highly developed
Color: Pale skin color

Research Ability

Line Pattern: Head line dips down into Luna mount
Length: Long head line
Mounts: High Saturn mount
Length: Long middle finger
Line Pattern: Small horizontal line at base of middle finger
Shape: Square fingertips

Reserved

Flexibility: Stiff hands
Length: Long fingers, long thumb
Gestures: Thumb held close to hand
Consistency: Palm medium-firm to hard, with
Length: Long middle finger
Line Pattern: Narrow arc to life line

Resilient

Length: Long, deep life line
Line Pattern: Double life line
Mounts: High, firm Venus mount
Mounts: Strong, firm Upper and Lower Mars mounts
Size: Medium thick or thick hands, with no "hollow" in center of palm
Size: Thin palms, with
Flexibility: Very flexible fingers

Resourceful

Flexibility: Very supple fingers bend backwards easily
Length: All fingers of balanced length
Mounts: All upper mounts highly developed (firm and pink)
Length: Little finger is average-to-long in length

Responsible

Length: Long middle finger, with
Mount: High Saturn mount
Length: Long thumb, with
Flexibility: Thumb offers some resistance to touch
Line Pattern: Strong, long fate line, with no defects on it
Mounts: Upper Mars mount highly developed

Shape: Square-shaped palms
Line Pattern: Straight head line

Responsive

Line Pattern: Curved heart and head lines, with
Color: Pink palms
Line Pattern: Fate line starts on Luna mount, continues on to Saturn mount
Consistency: Soft palms
Gestures: Fingers held wide apart

Result-oriented

Shape: Square-shaped hands, nails, and fingertips
Line Pattern: Straight head line
Length: Long thumb
Consistency: Firm palm
Size: Thick base to palm
Shape: Spatulate-shaped palms

Rigid

Flexibility: Stiff fingers
Gestures: Fingers held close together
Gestures: Fingers curve in toward palm when hand is held upright
Flexibility: Stiff thumb that does not move when pressure is applied
Consistency: Very hard palm

Risk Taker

Flexibility: Fingers very flexible
Gestures: Fingers held wide apart
Shape: Spatulate-shaped palms and nails
Gestures: Thumb held at a wide angle away from palm
Length: Long ring fingers

Psychic

Resilient

Reasonable

Reserved

Research Ability

Sad

Romantic

Line Pattern: Heart line deep, curved or forked at the end

Line Pattern: Heart line ends on Jupiter mount, especially with a triple-prong fork

Mounts: High, firm Venus mount

Sad

Line Pattern: Heart line ends turned down under index finger

Color: Yellow or pale-colored palms

Line Pattern: Drooping branches on heart line

Line Pattern: Head line ends on Luna mount, with

Line Pattern: Stress lines crossing the palm in a random pattern

Safety Conscious

Length: Long middle finger

Length: Long fingers, with

Shape: Square-shaped tips

Shape: Square-shaped palm

Gestures: Fingers held close together

Flexibility: Stiff fingers (naturally occurring, not result of arthritis or injury)

Sales Ability

Line Pattern: Head line begins widely separated from life line

Shape: Round or spatulate-shaped palms

Mounts: Well-developed Lower Mars mount (initiative)

Mounts: Firm, well-developed upper Mars mount (follow-through)

Line Pattern: Fate line starts on Luna mount

Color: Pink color on palm

Scholarly

Length: Long middle finger, long little finger

Mounts: Well-developed Saturn and Mercury mounts

Length: All fingers long

Size: Thin hands

Scientific Ability

Mounts: Strong Saturn and Mercury mounts

Shape: Square-shaped fingers and palms

Line Pattern: Straight head line

Line Pattern: Long head line, ending under ring or little finger

Special Feature: Long middle phalange on middle finger

Special Feature: Long bottom phalange on middle finger

Length: Long little finger

Secretive

Gestures: Fingers held close together, or **bending in toward palm**

Finger: Little finger curls inward toward palm (if not result of injury)

Line Pattern: Head line starts inside life line

Line Pattern: Life line has narrow arc, with

Color: Pale-colored palms

Line Pattern: Straight, short head line

Secure

Gestures: Fingers held wide apart in confident posture
Flexibility: Flexible fingers
Mounts: All mounts firm and well-developed
Line Pattern: Absence of stress lines on palm

Security-minded

Consistency: Soft hands
Length: Long palms
Size: Thin palms
Flexibility: Stiff fingers
Gestures: Fingers curl in toward palms
Mounts: Strong Saturn mount
Length: Long middle finger
Line Pattern: Long, straight fate line, centered in middle of palm

Self-assertive

Length: Long index finger and thumb
Mounts: Highly developed Lower Mars mount
Size: Fleshy, thick hands and fingers

Self-confident

Line Pattern: Head line begins widely separated from life line
Mounts: Highly developed Jupiter mount
Gestures: Fingers spread wide apart when gesturing
Gestures: Thumb held at a wide angle away from hand
Flexibility: Fingers flexible at their base where they join palm

Self-controlled

Size: Large thumb
Length: Long thumb
Line Pattern: Straight head line
Length: Long middle finger
Mounts: Strong Saturn mount
Flexibility: Thumb and fingers held stiffly, do not flex easily

Self-disciplined

Shape: Square hands
Line Pattern: Straight head line
Consistency: Firm palm
Line Pattern: Long, straight fate line
Length: Fingers average length, not short

Sensitive

Texture: Very fine skin
Size: Thin hands
Line Pattern: Many fine lines crossing the palm surface
Line Pattern: A grille or cross-hatch pattern on Lower Mars mount
Line Pattern: Head line starts inside life line, on Lower Mars mount
Line Pattern: Breaks in head or heart lines

Sentimental

Line Pattern: Long, curved heart line, with numerous branches
Mounts: Large Venus mount
Color: Pink Venus mount
Line Pattern: Horizontal lines on Venus mount
Line Pattern: Head line dips down into Luna mount

Serious
Length: Long middle finger
Mount: Well-developed Saturn mount
Shape: Any square shape, on palm, nails, or fingertips

Single-minded
Line Pattern: Straight head line
Line Pattern: Short, deep head line
Length: Long thumb
Consistency: Hard palm

Skeptical
Length: Long middle finger, long little finger
Line Pattern: Narrow space between head and heart lines
Color: Yellow tone to skin

Slow
Length: Long fingers
Special Feature: Knotted knuckles (finger joints enlarged)
Line Pattern: Head line dips down into Luna
Special Feature: Composite (double loop) fingerprint on thumb tip

Sociable
Shape: Round palm, fingertips, and nails
Mount: Large, well-formed Venus mount
Line Pattern: Curved heart line, ending up high between index and middle fingers

Color: Pink coloring on palm
Mounts: Well-developed upper mounts
Length: Long ring finger

Specialist
Line Pattern: Short, straight head line
Shape: Square-shaped nails and palm
Mounts: Large Saturn mount
Length: Long middle finger

Spontaneous
Flexibility: Very flexible fingers
Gestures: Wide space between fingers
Line Pattern: Head line widely separated from life line
Shape: Round fingertips, round palm
Color: Pink on palm
Size: Medium-thick or thick palm

Steadfast
Shape: Square-shaped hands, fingertips, and nails
Line Pattern: Straight or slightly curved head line
Line Pattern: Head line drawn clear, with no marks or defects
Line Pattern: Long, deep fate line

Strategizer
Finger: Index finger curves slightly to the side, toward middle finger
Length: Long little finger
Mounts: Large Jupiter mount

Sad

Secretive

Scientific Ability

Slow

Scientific Ability

Stressed

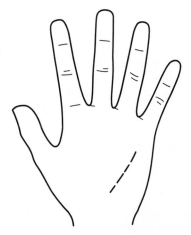

Stressed

Line Pattern: Broken Mercury line
Line Pattern: Many fine lines crossing the palm
Mounts: Flat Upper Mars mount (flat outside edge of hand)
Special Feature: Hollow palm (center of palm dips in middle, like a bowl)
Consistency: Very soft palms

Strong

Line Patterns: All lines deep, clear
Consistency: Firm palms
Length: Long thumb
Length: All finger lengths balanced, and in proportion to each other
Line Pattern: No stray lines cutting across the palm

Submissive

Consistency: Soft hands
Size: Thin hands
Length: Short thumb
Flexibility: Very flexible thumb
Line Pattern: Head line begins chained and tied to life line

Suggestible

Flexible: Fingers very flexible in all their joints
Shape: Pointed fingertips
Mounts: Large, long Luna mount, bulges near wrist

Sympathetic

Shape: Round-shaped palms, nails, and finger tips

Color: Pink coloring on palm
Line Pattern: Curved heart line
Mounts: All mounts well-developed

Talented

Mounts: Mounts are major indicators of talent:
Jupiter Mount: Leadership and community service
Saturn Mount: Science and research
Apollo Mount: Creativity and the arts
Mercury Mount: Communication, psychology, teaching, business
Lower Mars Mount: Medicine, surgery, and sales
Upper Mars Mount: Athletics, the military, security matters
Luna Mount: Drama, literature, nature studies, leisure industry
Venus Mount: Home matters, raising pets, decorating, dancing, music
A large, firm mount, with pink coloring, means that mount's talents are developed
Line Pattern: A good Apollo line also indicates talent

Talkative

Line Pattern: A long, wavy head line
Special Feature: Whorl (peacock's eye) fingerprints
Mounts: Strongly developed Mercury mount

Temper

Color: Red color on the whole palm, and red lines
Line Pattern: Head line starting on Lower Mars mount
Finger: Very thick thumb tip
Line Pattern: Numerous stress lines across palm

Temperamental

Length: Finger length uneven, one finger much longer or shorter than average
Line Pattern: Wavy head or heart line, one or more major lines has a break
Line Pattern: Chained heart and head lines
Line Pattern: Islands on the major lines
Line Pattern: Head and heart line combined into one line (Simian line)
Line Pattern: Lower prong of forked heart line droops, touches head line

Tenacious

Mounts: Full Upper Mars mount
Line Pattern: Straight, deep head line
Length: Long thumb
Line Pattern: Deep lines, especially the life line

Timid

Line Pattern: Head and life lines joined or chained at their beginning
Line Pattern: Head line begins inside life line
Line Pattern: Narrow arc to life line
Mounts: Flat Venus mount
Color: Pale color on palm

Line Pattern: Very small space between head and heart lines

Touchy

Color: White or pale-colored palms
Consistency: Soft palms
Texture: Fine skin
Line Pattern: Crossbars on major lines
Line Pattern: Grille pattern on Venus mount

Tough

Consistency: Firm or hard palm, with
Line Pattern: Few, deep lines, with
Mounts: Full Upper Mars mount
Length: Long thumb
Size: Thick, large thumb
Mounts: Strongly developed Venus mount

Tranquil

Line Pattern: Deep, clear life line
Line Pattern: Absence of stray lines across the palm
Line Pattern: No breaks in major lines
Mounts: Good Saturn and Apollo mounts

Travel, Love Of

Line Pattern: Wide arc to life line
Line Pattern: Life line swings away from Venus mount to end on Luna mount
Mounts: Large Luna mount
Line Pattern: Branch from life line swings over to Luna mount
Line Pattern: Series of short horizontal lines on outside edge of hand

Trusting

Line Pattern: Curved heart line, with
Color: Pink color on palm
Mounts: Well-developed Jupiter mount
Line Pattern: Wide space between head
    and heart lines
Flexibility: Flexible thumb and fingers

Trustworthy

Fingers: All fingers straight, not
    crooked, unless injured
Fingers: Little finger is very straight,
    not curved or bent inward
Line Pattern: Clear, deep, well-formed
    head line
Line Pattern: Head and heart lines free
    from islands, breaks, or bar lines

Truthful

Fingers: Straight little finger, not
    curved or bent inward
Length: Average length little finger
Line Pattern: Head line does not fork
    deeply into the Luna mount

Unbalanced

Size: Any feature out of proportion—
    e.g., thick hand, thin fingers
Length: Any finger very long or very
    short
Color: Any extreme in color—hand too
    pale or too red
Consistency: Any extreme—hands too
    soft or too hard

Unbending

Consistency: Very hard palm, with
Flexibility: Very stiff fingers, with
Line Pattern: Very few lines, only the
    main lines
Color: Red palm
Size: Thick, badly formed thumb
Line Pattern: Very straight, deep head
    line

Uncertain

Line Pattern: Wavy head or heart line
Line Pattern: Fate line fades in and out
    on its course along the palm
Consistency: Soft palm, with
Mounts: Flat Upper Mars mount
Shape: Hollow palm (bowl-like dip in
    center of palm)
Special Feature: Composite (double
    loop) thumbprint
Special Feature: Composite print on any
    other finger

Uncommunicative

Mounts: All upper mounts flat or
    under-developed
Mounts: Flat Mercury mount
Flexibility: Stiff hands
Color: Pale palms
Line Pattern: Narrow arc to life line

Unpredictable

Line Pattern: Wavy head and heart
    lines
Line Pattern: Uneven space between
    head and heart lines

Line Pattern: Islands on heart or head line

Line Pattern: Bar lines cutting the heart or head line

Unpretentious

Length: Slightly short index finger
Size: Thin palms
Size: Thin fingers with wide spaces at base where fingers join palm
Length: Short or average length ring finger, with
Mounts: Flat Venus mount

Unreasonable

Size: Thick second section of the thumb (between tip and ball of thumb)
Size: Very thick thumb
Consistency: Very hard palms, with
Flexibility: Stiff fingers
Mounts: Very large Jupiter mount

Upbeat

Line Pattern: Curved heart line
Color: Pink color on palm
Line Pattern: Deep life line, curved in a wide arch
Line Pattern: Long fate line, without breaks, islands, or bar lines on it
Line Pattern: Head line even in depth, no bar lines or other defects

Vacillating

Line Pattern: Head line wavy across the length of the palm
Line Pattern: Head line faintly drawn in hand

Line Pattern: Islands or breaks in the head line

Line Pattern: Head line dips deeply down into Luna mount

Length: Short thumb, with

Flexibility: Very flexible thumb

Flexibility: Flexible fingertips, with

Consistency: Soft palms

Vehement

Length: Long thumb, with
Size: Thick thumb, with
Line Pattern: Very straight head line
Mounts: Large Jupiter mount, with
Length: Very long index finger

Venturesome

Shape: Spatulate-shaped palms, nails, and fingertips
Gestures: Wide space between thumb and rest of hand
Gestures: Thumb held away from hand, pointed upward, as person talks
Size: Thick palms
Consistency: Firm palms

Verbal

Mounts: Large, well-developed Mercury mount
Length: Long little finger
Line Pattern: Long head line
Mounts: All upper mounts developed, with
Line Pattern: Long Apollo line

Versatile

Flexibility: Flexible fingers that bend easily
Shape: Spatulate-shaped palm, nails, and fingertips
Finger: Ring finger is very straight and long

Vigorous

Consistency: Firm or hard hands
Shape: Spatulate-shaped palms and nails
Mounts: Well-developed Venus mount
Mounts: Center of hand (Plain of Mars) well-developed, not hollow
Mounts: Upper Mars mount well-developed
Line Pattern: All major lines clear and deep
Size: Thick fingers

Visionary

Mounts: Large, full Luna mount
Mounts: Luna mount bulges at the wrist
Line Pattern: A triangle mark on Luna mount
Line Pattern: An "x" connecting the head and heart lines in center of hand, with
Mount: Large Mercury mount, with
Shape: Pointed fingertips
Line Pattern: Diagonal lines on Luna mount

Vital

Consistency: Firm palms
Color: Pink color on palms
Finger: Long, well-shaped thumb
Line Pattern: Long head, heart, and life lines, clear and free of defects

Vivacious

Mounts: Large Mercury and Venus mounts
Length: Short fingers
Flexibility: Fingers all flexible
Gestures: Fingers held wide apart
Line Pattern: Very curved heart line
Line Pattern: Long heart line

Warm-hearted

Consistency: Soft hands, with
Line Pattern: Curved heart line
Mounts: Strong Apollo and Venus mounts
Color: Pink palms
Line Pattern: Curved head line, with
Line Pattern: Fate line starts on Luna mount

Weary

Consistency: Very soft hands, with
Color: Very pale hands
Shape: Center of palm sunken-looking
Line Pattern: Life or head lines chained, lightly etched in hand
Line Pattern: Major lines have breaks, islands, or other defects
Line Pattern: Random fine lines criss-crossing the palm

Talkative

Uncertain

Temper

Witty

Timid

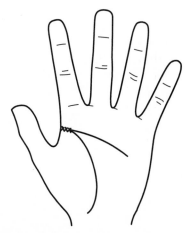

Welcoming
Mounts: All upper mounts well-developed, with
Consistency: Medium soft or soft hands
Shape: Round-shaped palm, nails, and fingertips
Color: Pink color on palms and nails
Line Pattern: Curved head and heart lines

Willful
Size: Very thick thumb tip
Flexibility: Stiff, inflexible thumbs
Mounts: Overly large Lower Mars mount
Mounts: Lower Mars mount firm, with
Line Pattern: Many small lines crossing the Lower Mars mount
Consistency: Hard palm, with
Length: A long index finger or thumb

Willing
Flexibility: Very flexible hands
Mounts: All mounts high and firm
Color: Pink coloring in palm
Line Pattern: Fate line long, deep, and clear, with no defective marks
Flexibility: Thumb flexible at base where it joins the palm

Will power
Length: Long, well-contoured thumb
Consistency: Firm palms
Line Pattern: Deep, clear, straight head line
Line Pattern: Double life line (a parallel second line inside the life line)

Wise
Mounts: Well-developed Saturn mount
Mounts: Average or slightly large Jupiter mount
Length: Average-to-long middle finger
Line Pattern: Deep head and heart lines
Line Pattern: Strong, long fate line
Special Feature: All features in hands (size, length) in proportion to each other

Withdrawn
Size: Thin palms, with
Color: Pale palms
Line Pattern: Narrow life line, with
Mounts: Flat Venus mount
Line Pattern: Fuzzy or faint appearance to head line

Witty
Mounts: Large Mercury mount
Length: Long Mercury finger
Line Pattern: Head line ends in a fork
Special Feature: "Humor" loop in skin ridges between ring and little fingers

Work-oriented
Shape: Very square shape on palms, nails, and fingertips
Length: Long thumb
Mounts: Strong Saturn mount
Length: Long middle finger
Line Pattern: Long, straight fate line
Consistency: Firm palms

Worldly

Shape: Wide base to palm
Mounts: Well-developed Venus, Luna, and Mars mounts
Size: Thick palms
Size: Thick fingers
Length: Long index finger

Worrier

Size: Thin, flat hands
Shape: Hollow palm (hand dips in the center)
Line Pattern: Numerous fine lines running across palm, cutting through life line
Consistency: Very soft palm

Writer

Mounts: Large, well-developed Mercury mount
Length: Long little finger
Line Pattern: Head line forks, one prong dips down into Luna mount
Line Pattern: An "x" beneath the heart line in the area under the little finger

Yielding

Consistency: Soft hands
Flexibility: Very flexible thumbs
Length: Short thumbs
Size: Thin palms, thin fingers, with
Line Pattern: Curved heart and head lines
Line Pattern: Faintly drawn fate line

Zealous

Color: Red color on the whole palm
Line Pattern: Head line begins widely separated from the life line
Mounts: All mounts full and large
Length: Long index finger

Good Hands and Bad Hands

So many palmistry books refer to good hands and bad hands. This topic is raised solely for the purpose of analysis, and to help in distinguishing the application of various qualities.

As it turns out, this topic also seems to be a preoccupation of people who want their hands analyzed. Anxiously they ask, "Do I have a good hand?"

Let's pause for a moment and see what the books mean when they refer to a "good hand."

This means a hand in which all the signs are balanced. One finger alone is not longer than the rest, one mount is not dominant, a pale color signifying introversion or lack of emotional warmth is not found in combination with a coarse skin, which signifies aggressive energies and physical strength. The fingers are straight; the head line deep and clear, and the thumb is well formed. Spacing between the fingers matches the degree of flexibility in the fingers.

For a quick and practical reference, here is a description of a good hand. If you find all these signs, it is a good hand indeed. The presence of any of these signs points the way to a person with real potential.

The heart line has been omitted from this list, for if the other qualities are there, they will guide the happiness and fulfillment of the person:

- Self-assurance, which is seen in a straight Jupiter finger of average or better length.
- Interests and talents, shown in good mount development accompanied by a firm texture.
- Concentration, found in a deep head line or in a balance between the mount development in each of the four zones of the hand.
- Balance in the finger sections, which indicates versatility.
- Complementary color and skin texture, which means that neither extreme of skin texture is accompanied by extremes in color.
- Motivation, seen in a good fate line that starts low in the hand and continues at least to the head line.
- Ability to reach goals, indicated by a well-formed thumb that is long or average in length.

Invariably, people ask, "Will you tell me the bad part?" The answer is, "Yes," of course, so long as the information is communicated in the spirit of concern and with an eye to preventing further difficulties.

Any sign of weak health and vitality should be noted and understated, put delicately, so as not to scare the person, but to make him or her aware that some area of their health should be guarded and checked.

Any sign of lowered motivation should be mentioned and corrected, and an inability to concentrate or a tendency to have "too many irons in the fire" will have to be remedied to promote growth and achievement.

Most definitely, any signs of a weak ego or a poor self-image have to be discussed. Support must be given and continued as necessary until the person learns and believes in his or her own worth.

Palmistry in itself can accomplish this miracle of support, for the gift of awareness is the biggest gift to be given. Once an external stimulus, the palmist, has touched the inner resources of another, these resources can be brought to life.

❧❧❧

Hand Print Analysis Examples

*T*he beauty of palmistry is that just a few clues from the hands are enough to paint a very insightful portrait of a person. A hand analysis can be as complicated or as simple as the number of clues chosen from among all the possible points of analysis.

Here we see three different hand prints, each one offering a look at the person's motivation and orientation to life, as revealed by the hands.

For each print, we will first assemble a list of features selected from all the possible clues in the hand, and give an overview of the personality using that list. To offer further insight into the person, we will take two or three or so of the clues at a time, combining them for a mini-analysis of the person.

EXAMPLE 1

Selected Features

- Large hands
- Thick third sections on the phalanges of the fingers
- A "detective" line at the base of the middle finger
- A wide space between the ring and little fingers
- Perfectionist loop
- Humor loop
- Curved heart line
- Drooping branches on the heart line
- Wide space between head and heart lines
- Forked head line
- Wide arc to life line
- Forked life line
- Fate line starts in center of palm
- Travel lines
- Full, large Luna mount
- Looped skin ridge patterns on Luna mount
- Squares on the Jupiter and Venus mounts

These seventeen clues will tell us quite a bit about this person. First, we see the mini-analysis, combining two or moe of the clues from our list, to get that quick insight into the person. Because the hands speak for the person, each analysis is written as if the hands themselves were talking out loud, to verbalize their message for the person.

Mini-Analysis

Describe this person	By combining these clues:
"I like to dance!"	Full Venus mount; full Luna mount
"I really love to be outdoors, nature is great!"	Full Luna mount, with looped skin ridge patterns

Example 1

"I easily find out what I need to know by going with the flow"	Wide hand; full Venus mount; forked head line; detective line at the bottom of the middle finger
"People often make me happy, I love to have a laugh and joke around"	Curved heart line; wide space between head and heart lines; humor loop
"Although in the past I have occasionally been disappointed in a relationship"	Drooping branches on heart line
"Adventure is my middle name, I like to spend my energy on a variety of activities"	Wide arc life line; life line forked at the end; travel lines; wide space between ring and little fingers; thick third sections on fingers
"However, I won't spread myself too thin; there's so much to do, I will choose a project to begin, and see it through to the end."	Straight fate line begins in the center of the palm; perfectionist loop; squares on Venus mount

A condensed statement from all the clues in the list would read:

Overview

"I want my presence on earth to make an impression. I'm so vital and full of life. Fun and adventure call my name, and I'll share the delight I find in life."

Here's a summary of all the clues in the selected list:

Overview

"My dreams and inner life work in consonance with opportunities that open up in a most serendipitous way. Potential in the here and now expands in a measured pace, leading to fulfillment of exciting future goals."

EXAMPLE 2

Selected Features

- Little fingertip curves toward ring finger
- Index finger leans toward middle finger
- Slightly short index finger
- Large thumb
- Perfectionist loop
- Forked heart line
- Curved head line
- Heart line in two sections, one section touches the head line
- Rising lines from the head line onto the Jupiter mount
- Head line touches life line
- Head line forked, with one prong on Luna mount
- Strong fate line changes course in the space between the head and heart lines

Mini-Analysis

Describe this person

"I am cautious, conscientious, and service-oriented, wanting to help others wherever I can. In the process, though, I don't lost sight of my own goals. Accomplishing what I set out to do is most important to me."

"I enjoy people, especially those with good ideas, and I like to debate the merits of those ideas"

"Each and every constructive thing I learn is indelibly engraved

By combining these clues:

Long thumb; index finger leans toward middle finger; slightly short index finger; head line touches life line; rising lines on Jupiter mount

Curved heart line; forked head line, Entire head line slopes toward Luna, with one prong of the fork on Luna; perfectionist loop; rising lines on Jupiter mount

Entire head line slopes toward Luna, with one prong of the fork on Luna;

Example 2

in my mind, and I build easily on my past experience, making the most of my opportunities"

perfectionist loop; rising lines on Jupiter mount

"Here's a clear record that I faced an important crossroads once in my life; I met the challenge and came out stronger for the experience"

Heart line in two sections, with one section touching the head line under the middle finger; fate line changes course in the space between the heart and head lines; and grows stronger above the heart line

"I treasure the people in my life, and all the occasions that we celebrate on our path together; holidays are important to me; I honor the ones I love and hold dear their memory"

Curved heart line; forked heart line; oblong palm

Here's a summary of all the clues in the selected list:

Overview

"My dreams and inner life work in consonance with opportunities that open up in a most serendipitous way. Potential in the here and now expands in a measured pace, leading to fulfillment of exciting future goals."

EXAMPLE 3

Selected Features

- Strong thumb
- Upper Mars mount developed
- Vertical lines on Mercury mount
- Two deep small lines form ring around base of index finger (Ring of Solomon)
- Additional section of heart line, up between the index nd middle fingers
- Slightly wavy heart line under middle finger
- Narrow space between head and heart line widens under ring finger
- Heart line sends branch to Apollo line, intersects another diagonal line, making a large triangle under the ring finger
- Island near beginning of head line
- Very well developed Luna mount
- Whorl pattern on Luna mount
- Small island on fate line near bottom of palm
- Life line branches, heads toward Luna, cutting through fate line
- Parallel line inside life line (Mars line)

Mini-Analysis

Describe this person

"People have taught me so much; just when I think I have people figured out, I discover another layer to a person, or another side to a personal situation; I value what I've learned, and I enjoy analyzing every situation that puzzles me; knowledge is the pearl of great price"

By combining these clues:

Additional section of heart line between index and middle fingers; narrow space between head and heart lines widens under ring finger; heart line slightly wavy under middle finger; two small deep lines form ring around base of index finger (called the Ring of Solomon, meaning wisdom in understanding people)

Example 3

"I would make a very good counselor teaching people the joys of accessing their own creativity, fun and for profit"

Vertical lines on Mercury mount; Ring of Solomon under index finger; heart line sends branch to Apollo line, for for intersecting another diagonal line from Mercury area, making a large triangle under the ring finger

"A little part of my childhood is a blur; I think I spent hours dreaming and then creating my own reality while someone around me worked out a challenge in their life"

Island near beginning of the head line; small island on fate line near bottom of palm

Mini-Analysis

Describe this person

"I love natural cycles and rhythm, music, magic, and mystery. I bring form to many of the creations that flow freely from my unconscious mind"

By combining these clues:

Very well developed Luna mount; whorl pattern on Luna mount; Upper Mars developed; strong thumb

"Once the course of my life appears set, changes unexpectedly creep in; nothing is set in stone; I move forward and enlarge my lifestyle in grand, sweeping vistas, especially after the age of forty-five"

Life line branches, heads toward Luna, cutting through the fate line; parallel line inside life line

Taken together, the clues in this hand might comment:

"There's so much to look forward to—if I keep up the pace, the joys and the lessons of my early years, I'll be something to reckon with! I'll travel, and when I'm home, I'll spend time in places that inspire me."

These three hand print samples are meant to demonstrate how the hands form a picture of a person in a life-giving way conducive to growth. May we always use the hands to point the way to self-fulfillment and generosity of spirit that adds to the harmony on earth.

APPENDIX 2

༺ঔৣঔ༻

Note to Readers

*I*n this work, you will have noticed a steady insistence on care, tact, and caution. We looked at a few of the stereotypes of palmistry and cases of misinformation that could be transmitted if the palmist were not careful.

I stress the cautious approach because without care, even hand readers who have the best of intentions can slip into a trap of presenting information that might alarm the listener.

This particular concern with a cautious approach to palmistry comes from personal experience. On occasion, people ask how I became interested in palmistry. The answer is that a well-meaning reader in Spain once looked at my hands and predicted: "At thirty-two you will lose everything you ever loved or owned, but you will survive. You will go on from there."

That was the appointment with destiny I thought I had until I became curious enough to investigate a palmistry book or two. Fortunately the Spanish woman had shown me the line that signified such drastic news to her.

It could be said that such an introduction to palmistry gave me motivation to find a reasonable explanation, not just for the line on my own hand, but, as an extension of that early search, for a rationale for the meanings of all signs in the hands.

Ironically, the point of the early reading that inspired my search into palmistry and the possible fears conveyed by the initial contact with palmistry made an apparent impact—for once this book was published, I discovered I had omitted the description of that very line! Thus, it occurs to me that often we are the best illustration of our own stories and preoccupations.

To make the story and this book complete, I would like to add here a consideration of the meanings of a broken line, whether it be a major or minor line, which signals an interruption in the free expression of the energy that the line represents. Traditionally, a broken head line is said to show nervousness, a high-strung nature, and possible injury to the head. In my own case, I was very impressed when I read the latter meaning, for the summer before the trip to Spain I was in an accident in which the worst injury was a blow to the head.

Experience has shown me that while the original meanings of a broken head line are valid, this line, as well as others, can benefit from a wider consideration of their probable significance. A large part of the lines' significance stems from their location in the hand, and the mounts involved will help define each individual line's meaning. A combination of appropriate meanings helps to give a complete picture.

Interestingly, most breaks in the head line occur under the Saturn mount. This mount's meaning concerns a search for wisdom, maturity, and values. The head line represents the ability to concentrate. If the head line is broken, the ability to concentrate is interrupted. How this interruption will be expressed depends upon the location of the break, as well as the individual's predisposition.

In a sense, with a head line broken under Saturn, we might expect to find a person who has gotten derailed at one point in his or her search for constant values and meanings in life. A person with a broken head line tends to find him- or herself in crises—in the sense of turning points—at some stage in their life, usually in the early thirties, in which a thorough overhaul of their life seems a pressing issue. Goals must be rearranged, marriage or career re-evaluated, and above all, the person's current situation must be found to have value and depth.

Broken head lines often correspond to an intense questioning of the role-playing, conventions, and expected demands made by the concepts of various stages of growth. Broken head lines can mean debating issues longer than necessary, and so the person may be indecisive. This attitude can also foster an extreme response to pressures—hence the traditional meaning of "high-strung" would be valid.

A broken head line can denote a period of strain in a person's life. This strain can be a result of inner needs or outer circumstances. More study needs to be done and records kept of the developments in the lives of those with broken head lines.

A word of counsel to those who have broken head lines would be to prepare for periods of indecisiveness, perhaps for disruptions in the planned course of life or for major re-evaluation of what has been learned, but all with the reassurance that the line itself in no way signifies catastrophe.

Breaks on the head line follow the same pattern as on all lines: the break can be clean or the ends can overlap. This last configuration is the more common of the two.

With an overlapping break, a more gradual transition in thought takes place, while the clean break shows a sudden awareness of a shift in thinking or an unexpected need to make a decision.

If we were to consider both breaks as an indication of some strain, we could say that the person with an ends-overlapping break would arrive at that point through response to a series of small issues, while the clean break would most likely denote an outer set of circumstances that suddenly causes the person to re-examine his or her life's direction. The most important factor to be aware of is that a broken head line need not be an issue of concern so much as a call to preparedness.

What is most interesting for palmists is that people are often aware of their hands just because they are different. This means a palmist will see quite a few broken head lines, short life lines, or single-line combinations of head and heart lines, known as the Simian line, all because the person asking has been made aware of their differences.

The palmist's greatest task is to put these differences into context, and that context is the person him- or herself—for palmistry is the art of the recognition of the individual.

⤳⟊⟊⟋⤵

A Brief Guide
for Further Study

For more information on steps you may take to self-fulfillment through awareness of your health, talents, and personality as reflected in your hands, the following books are recommended:

HEALTH

Your Life in Your Hands, Beryl B. Hutchison. London: Neville Spearman, 1967.

This book provides an essential understanding of the anatomy of the hand and how it relates to the interpretations of various areas of the hand. See this book for its chapters on physical and psychological health.

A Doctor's Guide to Better Health Through Palmistry, Eugene Scheimann, M.D. West Nyack, NY: Parker Publishing Co. Inc., 1969.

A practical book that is greatly enriched by a physician's experience in using hands as a diagnostic tool. The unique value of the hand as a supporting diagnostic tool for the physician opens exciting vistas for further scientific exploration of palmistry. Clues for achieving and maintaining good health through signs found in the hand are given.

TALENTS

The New Fortune in Your Hand, Elizabeth Daniels Squire. New York: Fleet Press Corporation, 1968.

This book contains a very informative history of palmistry and is lively in tone and presentation. It is particularly useful for studying specific signs of talent through the various configurations in the hands.

PERSONALITY

The Hand in Psychological Diagnosis, Charlotte Wolff. New York: Philosophical Library, 1952.

This book is recommended for a more technical, high-level professional guide to the personality as seen through the hands. Dr. Wolff brings considerable expertise to the field of hand analysis, as well as professional credentials in the field of psychology.

GENERAL

The Laws of Scientific Hand Reading, William G. Benham. New York: Duell, Sloan and Pierce, 1966.

This is the standard reference for all palmistry students. Many systems of hand analysis today owe a debt to the research of Benham. Recently this book was cited as slighting the needs of women, but it is very useful for the basics of palmistry, and the meanings given can be translated into the needs of the feminine psyche.

Palmistry Made Easy, Fred Gettings. North Hollywood, CA: Wilshire Book Company, 1973.

Fred Gettings is the author of several books on palmistry. In this book, the reader will find useful information on hand types and an abundant selection of prints. The book is geared toward an intuitive perception of the hand. Knowing the types of hands helps to differentiate the hands' qualities and to provide an understanding of the hand as a whole.

Palmistry for Women, Nancy MacKenzie. New York: Warner Paperback Library Edition, 1973.

A feminist approach to palmistry is presented in this book. This book is extremely useful as a guide to careers for women. Sample prints of women in various professions are given, as well as pertinent guidelines for career choices based on information provided by the hands.

Free Magazine

Read unique articles by Llewellyn authors, recommendations by experts, and information on new releases. To receive a **free** copy of Llewellyn's consumer magazine, *New Worlds of Mind & Spirit,* simply call 1-877-NEW-WRLD or visit our website at www.llewellyn.com and click on *New Worlds.*

LLEWELLYN ORDERING INFORMATION

Order Online:
Visit our website at www.llewellyn.com, select your books, and order them on our secure server.

Order by Phone:
- Call toll-free within the U.S. at 1-877-NEW-WRLD (1-877-639-9753). Call toll-free within Canada at 1-866-NEW-WRLD (1-866-639-9753)
- We accept VISA, MasterCard, and American Express

Order by Mail:
Send the full price of your order (MN residents add 7% sales tax) in U.S. funds, plus postage & handling to:

Llewellyn Worldwide
P.O. Box 64383, Dept. 0-7387-0756-2
St. Paul, MN 55164-0383, U.S.A.

Postage & Handling:
Standard (U.S., Mexico, & Canada). If your order is:
Up to $25.00, add $3.50
$25.01 - $48.99, add $4.00
$49.00 and over, FREE STANDARD SHIPPING
(Continental U.S. orders ship UPS. AK, HI, PR, & P.O. Boxes ship USPS 1st class. Mex. & Can. ship PMB.)

International Orders:
Surface Mail: For orders of $20.00 or less, add $5 plus $1 per item ordered. For orders of $20.01 and over, add $6 plus $1 per item ordered.

Air Mail:
Books: Postage & Handling is equal to the total retail price of all books in the order.
Non-book items: Add $5 for each item.

Orders are processed within 2 business days. Please allow for normal shipping time.
Postage and handling rates subject to change.

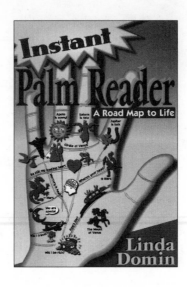

INSTANT PALM READER

A Road Map to Life
Linda Domin

Etched upon your palm is an aerial view of all the scenes you will travel in the course of your lifetime. Your characteristics, skills, and abilities are imprinted in your mind and transferred as images on to your hand. Now, with this simple, flip-through pictorial guide, you can assemble your own personal palm reading, like a professional, almost instantly.

The *Instant Palm Reader* shows you how your hands contain the picture of the real you—physically, emotionally, and mentally. More than 500 easy-to-read diagrams will provide you with candid, uplifting revelations about yourself: personality, childhood, career, finances, family, love life, talents, and destiny.

With the sensitive information artfully contained within each interpretation, you will also be able to uncover your hidden feelings and unconscious needs as you learn the secrets of this 3,000-year-old science.

1-56718-232-1, 256 pp., 7 x 10, illus.   **$14.95**

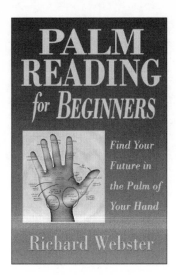

PALM READING FOR BEGINNERS

Find Your Future in the Palm of Your Hand

Richard Webster

Announce in any gathering that you read palms and you will be flocked by people thrilled to show you their hands. When you are have finished *Palm Reading for Beginners*, you will be able to look at anyone's palm (including your own) and confidently and effectively tell them about their personality, love life, hidden talents, career options, prosperity, and health.

Palmistry is possibly the oldest of the occult sciences, with basic principles that have not changed in 2,600 years. This step-by-step guide clearly explains the basics, as well as advanced research conducted in the past few years on such subjects as dermatoglyphics.

1-56718-791-9, 264 pp., 5³⁄₁₆ x 8, illus.   **$9.95**